Heroes of Bomber Command

SUFFOLK

GRAHAM SMITH

COUNTRYSIDE BOOKS
NEWBURY BERKSHIRE

Happy
Birthday,
Tim.

Lol

A

First published 2008
© Graham Smith, 2008

COUNTRYSIDE BOOKS
3 Catherine Road
Newbury, Berkshire

To view our complete range of books,
please visit us at
www.countrysidebooks.co.uk

ISBN 978 1 84674 103 6

Designed by Peter Davies, Nautilus Design
Produced through MRM Associates Ltd., Reading
Printed by Information Press, Oxford

All material for the manufacture of this book was
sourced from sustainable forests.

CONTENTS

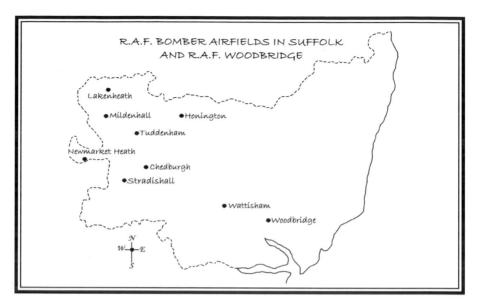

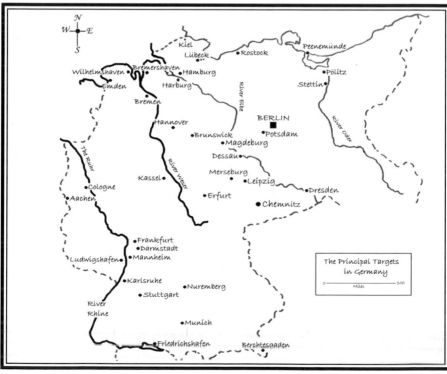

Introduction

It is now nearly seventy years since the men of Bomber Command started out on their long and harrowing war and at this distance of time it is a little difficult to comprehend the scale and immensity of the task that faced them, let alone the ordeals and terrors they encountered nightly for almost six years.

As a young schoolboy growing up during the Second World War I well recall sitting around the 'wireless' with my parents listening to the news night after night that 'the Royal Air Force bombed targets in Germany last night'. All those airmen were my heroes then but little did I realise the immense sacrifices they made in those dark and frightening years.

During the Second World War some one hundred and twenty-five thousand aircrew served in Bomber Command and of these fifty-five thousand, five hundred were killed, another eight thousand, four hundred wounded and over nine thousand, eight hundred made prisoners of war. This was a horrendous human sacrifice to pay for the Command's long and bitter strategic bombing offensive; Bomber Command's losses were over three-quarters of the Royal Air Force's total loss of airmen throughout the war.

Many flew from bomber stations in Suffolk and most were young; the average age was just twenty-two years. It is to those men of all ages that we all owe a deep debt of gratitude. It is difficult to find adequate words to express the immense contribution made by the men of Bomber Command, or indeed to describe their courage and bravery.

Since then I have been privileged to meet many veterans of Bomber Command, sadly now a rapidly diminishing number; each displayed a quiet and unassuming modesty almost to a fault, maintaining that they did 'nothing special, I was merely doing my duty'.

Air Chief Marshal Sir Arthur Harris, their most famous and celebrated Commander-in-Chief, likened it to 'the courage of the small hours with long drawn out apprehensions of "going over the top" ...'. He also said that, 'Such devotion must not be forgotten. It is unforgettable by anyone whose contacts gave them knowledge and understanding of what these young men experienced and faced'. To him they were 'the bravest of the brave'. To them he was 'The Chief' or 'Butch' and with a fierce and unswerving loyalty they would fly 'To Hell and Back' for him.

It is to the memory of those 'bravest of the brave' that I humbly dedicate this book; they were the real 'heroes' of Bomber Command

Graham Smith

Chapter 1

Enter Bomber Command

An aerial view of R.A.F. Mildenhall in September 1934. (via R. Roberts)

At the outbreak of war on 3rd September 1939 there were four established bomber stations in Suffolk – Mildenhall, Honington, Stradishall and Wattisham – along with a hastily requisitioned and makeshift airfield at Newmarket Heath. Some six years later, it was perhaps a little surprising to discover that despite all the urgency and hectic pace of aircraft construction within the county when twenty-two airfields were built, Bomber Command had only four *operational* airfields in Suffolk – Chedburgh, Mildenhall, Stradishall and Tuddenham.

Without a shadow of a doubt Suffolk was an integral part of what was known as 'bomber country' throughout the long and bitter air war, but the majority of these wartime airfields and two of the R.A.F.'s pre-war stations were occupied by combat groups of the United States Army Air Force in the guise of its Eighth Air Force. However, from the second day of the war right up to the final days in May 1945, Bomber Command crews from Suffolk airfields were in action, making a large and vital contribution to the Command's prolonged and costly battle.

The most prominent and well-known airfield in the county was, and indeed still is, Mildenhall. In the 1930s its fame was not just countrywide but worldwide. It had been constructed during 1933/4 on the edge of the Breckland about two miles north-west of the small town from whence it was named, although to most airmen that served there it was known simply as 'Beck Row' from the neighbouring village. When R.A.F. Mildenhall officially opened on 14th October 1934 under the command of Wing Commander F. J. Linnell, O.B.E., it was allocated to the A.O.C. (Air Officer Commanding) Western Area of the Air Defence of Great Britain, which then controlled both bomber and fighter squadrons. Mildenhall was one of the R.A.F.'s most modern and prestigious bomber stations – a veritable showplace for a confident and expanding Service.

A mere four days after its opening Mildenhall was used as the starting point for the 'MacRobertson Air Race' to Melbourne, Australia. All the celebrated aviators of the time were engaged in what was described as 'the world's greatest air race' and which received an immense amount of publicity. It was reported that over 70,000 people had gathered around the airfield to witness the start, hence the airfield's early fame. After all this heady euphoria it was somewhat of an anticlimax when Mildenhall received its first bomber squadron – No 99 – on 15th November 1934, which was destined to remain in Suffolk until March 1941.

The Squadron had been formed in August 1917, even then as a bomber squadron and part of the Independent Air Force (an early precursor of Bomber Command). It reformed in April 1924 again as a bomber unit and over the next ten years it had been equipped with a variety of bombers – Vimys, Aldershots, Hyderabads, and Hinaidis – but now with the

No 99 Squadron's badge, designed in 1934, was not formally approved by H.M. King George VI until December 1937.

R.A.F.'s latest heavy bomber, the Handley Page Heyford II. Indeed, it had been the first squadron to receive these new bombers at Upper Heyford in the previous November.

All R.A.F. stations and squadrons had their own badge or crest, a practice that was first introduced in 1936. The Squadron's badge had been designed in 1934 but it was not formally approved by H.M. King George VI until December 1937. It featured a black puma to represent its independence and night operations with the motto, *Quisque Tenax* or 'Each Tenacious'.

The crews' new aircraft was, like all R.A.F. aircraft of the time, a biplane, but a rather large one with a wing span of over 75 ft and twin Rolls-Royce Kestrel engines that gave a maximum speed of 142 mph and an operational range of some 900 miles with a maximum bomb load of 3,500 lbs. The Heyford possessed some unusual features: the upper wing was shoulder-mounted on the fuselage but the lower wing was some distance beneath the fuselage; one of its three gun stations, each armed with a 0.303 inch Lewis machine gun, was a retractable 'dustbin' gun turret under the fuselage; and part of its bomb load was carried in internal bomb cells – one of the first aircraft to be so equipped. The Heyford was a rather cumbersome and inelegant aircraft and, with its open cockpit and gun stations, it appeared not far removed from the lumbering giant bombers of the First World War. Although only one hundred and twenty-four Heyfords were produced, eleven squadrons were equipped with them, five of which still retained them well into 1939 and the aircraft was not declared obsolete until 1941. The Heyford was just one of a number of heavy bombers that flew from Suffolk airfields in the immediate war years.

On Saturday, 6th July 1935 Mildenhall was the venue for the first Royal

Review of the R.A.F. in honour of King George V's Silver Jubilee. Thirty-eight squadrons, comprising over three hundred and fifty aircraft (all biplanes), were drawn up in serried ranks in a great arc at this now famous airfield. H.M. The King, as the Chief of the R.A.F., accompanied by the Prince of Wales and the Duke of York, inspected the aircraft and over four thousand officers and airmen before motoring to R.A.F. Duxford where they later witnessed the largest flypast ever mounted; the one hundred and sixty-two aircraft from twenty squadrons were appropriately led by Heyfords of No 99 Squadron. After the successful review the King sent a personal message to the Service:

> I warmly congratulate all ranks of the R.A.F.... I was greatly impressed both by their smartness on the ground and their efficiency in the air, which leaves no doubt that they will prove fully equal to any task which they may be called upon to fulfil...

H.M. King George V at R.A.F. Mildenhall for the Jubilee Review of the Royal Air Force, 6th July 1935. (R.A.F. Museum)

Indeed, many of the airmen parading on this memorable day would be in action over four years later but not, of course, flying in the fighters and bombers on display!

On 1st September 'B' Flight of No 99 Squadron provided the nucleus of a newly reformed squadron – No 38. It could also date its origins back to the days of the Royal Flying Corps, in fact during July to September 1916 it was commanded by a certain Captain A.T. Harris, of later and lasting fame as C.-in-C. Bomber Command from 1942 to 1945. Needless to say, it was equipped with Heyfords but in November 1936 these were exchanged for Fairey Hendons and the Squadron remained at Mildenhall until May 1937 when it moved to R.A.F. Marham in Norfolk.

Although only fourteen Hendons were produced the aircraft deserves a special place in Bomber Command's history as the first all-metal low-wing monoplane to enter the Service. Its origins dated back to 1927 and it had first flown in November 1930 but was not ordered by the Air Ministry until five years later, by which time its low maximum speed (155 mph) and light bomb load (1,600 lbs) had made it virtually obsolescent. However, it was the first bomber to be designed with an internal bomb bay as well as guns in internal turrets. By January 1939 the Squadron had exchanged their Hendons for Wellingtons.

Largely as a result of the planned rapid and large expansion of the R.A.F., a radical and major reorganisation took place in 1936. The Air Defence of Great Britain was disbanded and replaced by four separate and functional Commands: Bomber, Fighter, Coastal and Training, each tasked with a precise and specific role and each divided into a number of Groups. Under the new system the individual Air Officer Commanding was responsible for his Command's planning and development, with the Chief of the Air Staff via the Air Ministry remaining in overall control of the operational policies.

Bomber Command was formed at Uxbridge on 14th May 1936 under the control of Air Marshal Sir John Steel and it subsumed the three Groups, Nos 1 to 3, which had been formed earlier in the year. Bomber Command was the logical and inevitable product of the R.A.F.'s presumed main role in a future war when during the 1920s and 1930s the concept of a powerful heavy bomber force striking into the heart of the enemy's territory was declared to be the main *raison d'etre* of the Service. The main and fiercest proponent of this doctrine was Sir Hugh Trenchard, Marshal of the Royal Air Force, who was once proclaimed as the 'patron saint of modern air power'. He was utterly convinced of this overwhelming heavy bomber force and was quite dismissive of the role of fighters, which would never be a match for heavy bombers, hence the reason why fighters were relegated to a minor role in the pre-war R.A.F.

The cult of the all-powerful bomber was further stressed in November 1932 when Stanley Baldwin, the Conservative politician and later Prime Minister, famously declared, 'there is no power on earth that can protect him [the man-in-the-street] from being bombed. Whatever people may tell him, *the bomber will always get through* [my italics]. The defence is offence'. Thus bomber squadrons outnumbered fighter squadrons by two to one and the bomber pilots were then considered the 'elite' of the R.A.F., almost a privileged class. In July 1936 there were 'just' two hundred and eighty bomber pilots of whom 70% were officers. Two years later the number had increased to over one thousand, three hundred and twenty, with the same percentage being commissioned officers.

Bomber Command's badge was not formally approved by H.M. King George VI until March 1947; the thunderbolt depicted on the badge represented the Command's striking force and the Astral Crown showed its success in the Second World War. The Command's motto, 'Strike Hard Strike Sure', has been retained by the R.A.F.'s present Strike Command, which was formed on 1st May 1968 with the amalgamation of Bomber and Fighter Commands.

The problems facing Air Marshal Sir John Steel in 1936 were quite formidable considering the expansion plans for his Command in the coming years: no 'real' modern bombers, an inadequate number of aircrew and trained groundcrew, an insufficient number of bomber airfields, poor equipment (the standard bomb was only 230 lbs) and a woeful lack of operational

Bomber Command's badge, with the Command's motto, 'Strike Hard, Strike Sure', was formally approved in March 1947.

training. However, it would be largely left to Air Chief Marshal Sir Edgar Ludlow-Hewitt, who took over as A.O.C.-in-C. Bomber Command on 12th September 1937, to develop and mould Bomber Command into a modern fighting force.

In January 1937 the Headquarters of No 3 Group moved from Andover to Mildenhall to be closer to the six airfields that would ultimately be allocated to the Group. Two new Groups of Bomber Command were also formed at Mildenhall, No 4 on 1st April 1937 and No 5 later in September; the former moved to Linton-on-Ouse, Yorkshire in June and the latter to Grantham, Lincolnshire in October. Also in April another squadron, No 149, reformed at Mildenhall, once again from airmen of 'B' Flight of No 99 Squadron. The Squadron dated back to March 1918 as a night-bomber unit hence its motto – *Fortis Nocte* or 'Strong by Night'. It was one of only two of the Command's squadrons to serve continuously during the Second World War. It was, of course, equipped with Heyfords and retained them until January 1939 when they were exchanged for Wellingtons. The Squadron would remain in Suffolk until May 1944, the longest serving bomber squadron in the county.

The second 'Expansion' (as they were known) bomber station to open in Suffolk was Honington on 3rd May 1937. It was sited about two miles to the west of the village and like Mildenhall it was placed in No 3 Group. Over two months later the first bomber squadrons arrived from Finningley, Yorkshire – Nos 102 and 77. The first was equipped with the inevitable Heyfords and the latter with Vickers Wellesleys.

In many ways the Wellesley was a quite remarkable day bomber. It was a single-engine monoplane and was the first of the Vickers aircraft to use the unusual and unique geodetic construction devised by Dr Barnes Wallis, of later 'bouncing bomb' fame. The design was claimed to provide maximum strength for minimum weight. The Wellesley's other unusual features were its twin cockpits and a very long wing. Although there were six Wellesley squadrons by the close of 1937, within a year all but one had been replaced by Wellingtons. The aircraft did, however, see active service in the Middle East and Africa. Its lasting claim to fame was that a flight of three Wellesleys of the R.A.F.'s Long-Range Development Flight made a record-breaking non-stop flight from Egypt to Australia in November 1938 – a quite remarkable distance of seven thousand, one hundred and sixty-two miles in just two days.

Air Chief Marshal Ludlow-Hewitt was under no illusions about the

These four pre-war bombers all flew from Suffolk airfields: 1. Handley Page Heyford; 2. Vickers Wellesley; 3. Fairey Hendon; 4. Handley Page Harrow.

massive problems that he and his Command faced. After an exhaustive tour of the stations and squadrons under his command, he reported in November: '[It] is entirely unprepared for war, unable to operate except in fair weather and is extremely vulnerable both in the air and on the ground'. 'Ludlow', as he was known in the Service, guided Bomber Command through its re-equipment and rapid pre-war expansion, and despite all its failings and shortcomings at the outbreak of war, the Command (and indeed the country) owes him a deep debt of gratitude,

Air Chief Marshal Sir Edgar Ludlow-Hewitt was A.O.C.-in-C. Bomber Command from September 1937 to April 1940. (R.A.F. Museum)

especially in respect of his brave and courageous decision in January 1939 to remove a number of his precious squadrons from operations to form 'Reserve' or 'Group Pool' squadrons for a proper and organised operational training and conversion regime.

With the benefit of hindsight it is difficult to comprehend why, on 19th October 1937, R.A.F. Mildenhall acted as host to a top-level German Air Force mission, which inspected the Heyfords of Nos 99 and 149 Squadrons along with other current R.A.F. aircraft – the Handley Page Harrow, Armstrong Whitworth Whitley, Vickers Wellesley and Bristol Blenheim – and other types of technical equipment. Amongst the high-ranking German party were General Erhard Milch, head of the German Air Force (*Luftwaffe*) and Generals Hans-Juergen Stumpff and Ernst Uder. It must have been rather galling for Ludlow-Hewitt to accompany this party and show them all his Command's latest bombers, especially as only days before he had received his copy of a report by senior members of the three Services

Air Chief Marshal Sir Edgar Ludlow-Hewitt with General Milch, Head of the German Luftwaffe, *at R.A.F. Mildenhall on 19th October 1937. (R.A.F. Museum)*

on their *Appreciation of the Situation in the Event of War against Germany in 1939*! Whether the fact that the aircrews had been specifically briefed to give misleading answers regarding the capabilities of their aircraft and equipment eased his mind is open to conjecture. The German officers were treated to a fly-past before they left to spend the night at the R.A.F. College at Cranwell. Less than two years later the two Air Forces would be opposing each other in battle.

The third new 'Expansion' station to be constructed in the county was mainly located in the parish of Hardon to the south of the A413 road and just a mile or so to the east of Stradishall, from whence it was named. It was officially opened on 3rd February 1938 under the command of Group Captain J.H. Henning, D.S.O., M.C., and of course it was placed in No

3 Group. The construction work had been undertaken by Sir Lindsey Parkinson & Co. Ltd. at a cost of £½ million. But because of the heavy clay, which caused considerable drainage problems, it was decided by the Air Ministry that the airfield would become the first in Bomber Command to be provided with hard runways. The work did not commence until late 1939, with the result that the airfield was not available for operations until January 1940.

The first two bomber squadrons to occupy R.A.F. Stradishall arrived in March 1938 – Nos 9 and 148 – equipped with Heyfords and Wellesleys respectively. As its number suggests, No 9 was the oldest squadron to serve in Suffolk. It had first been formed in December 1914 but it was disbanded within months, only to be reformed in April 1915 when its first Commander was Major H.C.T. Dowding, later to become Air Chief Marshal Sir Hugh Dowding, the A.O.C.-in-Chief of Fighter Command during the Battle of Britain. Like No 99 Squadron it had reformed back in 1924 as a heavy bomber unit. In November 1938 the Squadron lost their Commander in a tragic flying accident. Wing Commander Harry

No 9 Squadron's Wellingtons bearing their pre-war code 'KA'. It had received the new bombers in January 1939.

A. Smith, along with Pilot Officer A.W. Jackson, were both killed when their Heyford overshot the runway at Stradishall and burst into flames; he was replaced by Wing Commander H.P. Lloyd. But for a brief spell with Coastal Command during April 1940, the Squadron served with Bomber Command throughout the war.

In July 1938 when Nos 75 and 215 Squadrons arrived at Honington from Driffield, yet another new monoplane bomber made its appearance in the county – the Handley Page Harrow. It had first flown in October 1936 and had been originally designed as a troop transport. The aircraft was powered by two 925 hp Bristol Pegasus XX engines giving a maximum speed of 200 mph and an operational range of 1,250 miles. The Harrow was armed with four 0.303 inch Browning guns in three turrets and could carry 3,000 lbs of bombs. The bomber was really superseded by the Wellington and only one hundred were built; they were still in use in a transport role right up to May 1945, being affectionately known as 'Sparrows'.

Mildenhall recorded another claim to fame when, on 18th October 1938, No 99 became the first squadron to receive the Command's newest heavy bomber – the legendary Vickers-Armstrong Wellington. In retrospect when one considers the aircraft's performance in the Second World War, it was a most auspicious day not only for the Squadron and Mildenhall but also for Bomber Command.

The Wellington was a most remarkable bomber, fondly beloved by its crews and the public alike. Like the Wellesley it had been designed by Dr Barnes Wallis and was of the same geodetic lattice construction. Originally called Crecy in honour of the famous victory of 1346, its name was changed to Wellington after the 'Iron Duke'. It later acquired its popular nickname 'Wimpy' after J. Wellington Wimpy, a character in the popular *Popeye* newspaper cartoon. The prototype (K4049) had first flown on 15th June 1936 and production commenced in December 1937. It was powered by two Bristol Pegasus XVIII engines, giving a top speed of about 235 mph at 15,500 ft and it could carry a 4,500 lb bomb load; also it was the first bomber capable of carrying the 4,000 lb 'blockbuster' bomb. There were Frazer-Nash nose and tail turrets with twin 0.303 inch Browning guns, as well as two single Brownings in beam positions. One of No 99 Squadron's pilots claimed 'they brought a new era of military flying for the pilots of Bomber Command...it was something entirely new and very exciting' Certainly, at long last, Bomber Command had for the first time a true modern bomber and the Wellington became one of the outstanding aircraft of the Second World War.

At the outbreak of the war Bomber Command had one hundred and seventy-five Wellingtons on charge, all with the eight squadrons of 3 Group – six front-line and two reserve. These squadrons suffered the first heavy losses and during the early war years Wellingtons were the mainstay of Bomber Command and its night operations. Over forty-seven thousand, four hundred operational sorties were made by the Command's forty-five Wellington squadrons, only surpassed by Lancasters and Halifaxes; some one thousand, three hundred and eighty (2.9%) were lost in action. Over eleven thousand, four hundred and sixty Wellingtons were built, the largest number of any British bomber, and it became the ubiquitous bomber used for operational training; the majority of bomber crews received their training on Wellingtons and thus 'that old-fashioned Wimpy of mine' held a very special place in the hearts of all 'Bomber Men'.

In April 1937 the Air Ministry purchased an area of farmland to the east of the village of Wattisham and in just two years (5th April 1939) a new bomber station opened under the command of Group Captain Oswald Gayford, D.F.C., A.F.C. He was quite a celebrated officer, having specialised in long-distance flying since 1931 and five years later he was in command of the R.A.F.'s prestigious Long Distance Flight. The airfield at Wattisham was allocated to No 2 Group, one of the famous 'W' airfields in that Group, the others being Watton, West Raynham, and Wyton. Since the Group's formation back in March 1936 it had been given the control of Bomber Command's light bomber squadrons, which meant that two squadrons of Bristol Blenheims would soon arrive at the new airfield.

In early April No 107 Squadron arrived from Harwell, Berkshire followed in May by No 110 Squadron from Waddington, Lincolnshire. Both squadrons had originated in the First World War and had been reformed in 1936 and 1937 respectively, and they each brought a mixture of Blenheim Is and IVs to Wattisham; over the next three years Wattisham became one of the most famous 'Blenheim stations' in the Command, launching the first and last Blenheim bombing operations.

The Bristol Blenheim was another legendary aircraft of the Second World War; it spearheaded the Command's daylight operations in the early war years. The Bristol 142, as it was originally designated, made its maiden flight in April 1935. It had been built at the behest of Lord Rothermere, the proprietor of the *Daily Mail*; he named it *Britain First*. After the Air Ministry had shown an interest in the aircraft he generously donated it to the

Bristol Blenheim IVs: They first arrived at R.A.F. Wattisham in April 1939.

nation. However, the Bristol Aeroplane Company had already designed an improved military version – a twin-engine medium day bomber. The 142M was of all-metal construction, capable of carrying 1,000 lbs of bombs over a range of 1,125 miles at a top speed of 279 mph, which was then faster than any R.A.F. fighter. It required a three-man crew and was armed with a 0.303 inch machine-gun in the port wing and a Vickers 'K' gun in the dorsal turret. Its performance was so impressive that the Air Ministry immediately ordered one hundred and fifty 'off the drawing board', a rare occurrence in those days, to be quickly followed by another order for five hundred and seventy; obviously the Air Ministry felt that it had 'a winner' on its hands.

In May 1936 it was officially named the Blenheim I and the first example entered the Service in March 1937. Within months the Bristol Aeroplane Company had produced a more powerful model – the Type 149 which was intended as a reconnaissance aircraft for Bomber Command. It was provided with additional fuel tanks and larger Mercury XV engines, but the most striking difference was a lengthened nose – an extra three feet – which provided a position for the observer/radio operator ahead of and to the right of the pilot. When the prototype first flew in September 1937 it was called the Bolingbroke but this name was dropped when it was developed for Bomber Command and it was merely designated the Mark IV. The bomber now had an increased range of 1,460 miles but a slightly lower maximum speed of 266 mph; external racks were fitted to carry an additional 320 lbs of bombs and another 0.303 inch gun was fitted beneath the nose. The first Blenheim IVs entered the Service on 22nd March 1939 and by the outbreak of the war the R.A.F. had over one

Wellingtons of No 149 Squadron over Paris on 14th July 1939 (Bastille Day).

thousand Blenheims, more than any other type of aircraft, but less than two hundred were the improved Mark IVs.

Just weeks before the outbreak of war No 3 Group suffered a serious setback when its Air Officer Commanding, Air Commodore A.A.B. Thomson, was killed in a tragic accident on 8th August. He had flown from R.A.F. Marham to test an experimental bomb but problems with the bomb release mechanism forced the aircraft to land at Boscombe Down. Once they had landed the Air Commodore went to check the mechanism, when the bomb fell to the ground. In his rush to get away in case the bomb exploded, he was struck by one of the revolving propellers and was killed instantly. He was replaced on 29th August by Air Vice-Marshal J.E.A. 'Jack' Baldwin, who would remain in charge until mid-September 1942. Baldwin proved to be an inspiring leader and was very popular with his crews and occasionally flew operations with them, a practice strongly discouraged by Command headquarters. No 2 Group's Commander was Air Vice-Marshal C. Maclean, who had been in the post since May 1938. He was a New Zealander who had served in the Royal Flying Corps and he remained in charge of the Group until his retirement from the R.A.F. in May 1940.

Despite all the efforts and resources devoted to Bomber Command in the previous two years, it would be fair to say that the Command was somewhat ill-prepared for the air war ahead. Its crews, although highly professional and well trained in actual flying, had little experience of long-range flying, especially at night, and only a precious few had precise navigational skills. Furthermore their equipment was barely adequate: fuel tanks and systems were unprotected from enemy fire, as indeed were the pilots; heating for high-altitude flying was sadly inadequate; radios and bombing systems were unsatisfactory and their defensive armament was weak. The Official History – *The Strategic Air Offensive against Germany 1939-1945* – a three-volume work published in 1961, was rather forthright in its opinion:

> When war came in 1939 Bomber Command was not trained or equipped either to penetrate into enemy territory by day or to find its target areas, let alone its targets by night...[it] was above all an investment in the future.

It remained to be seen how Bomber Command and its brave and valiant crews would cope with what has since been described as 'the most continuous and gruelling operation of war ever carried out'.

Chapter 2

'A Few Harsh and Costly Lessons'

(1939)

On 1st September 1939, as a consequence of the German invasion of Poland, a general mobilisation of the Royal Air Force was ordered. Although Bomber Command then comprised fifty-three squadrons, ten were quickly despatched to France to form the Advanced Air Striking Force and twenty had been allocated for operational training as 'Group Pool' squadrons. Thus the Command was left with twenty-three operational squadrons in four Groups, barely two hundred and eighty aircraft, at just twenty-three operational airfields.

Before the expected War Telegram that 'War has broken out with Germany only' was sent out to all those airfields on the fateful Sunday morning two days later, the Command had found that the goalposts had suddenly been moved. In response to the appeal made by Franklin D. Roosevelt, the U.S. President, that Britain, France and Germany should refrain from bombing undefended towns and targets where civilians may be killed or injured, both France and Britain readily gave such assurances; therefore the Command's immediate and *only* target was now the German Fleet and furthermore solely whilst it was at sea. This action was the twelfth in a list of thirteen Western Air Plans that had been formalised in January 1939 as Bomber Command's war strategy, but on 1st September Air Chief Marshal Sir Edgar Ludlow-Hewitt received W.A.7(a) which ordered an air attack on the naval

Wellingtons of No 149 Squadron over R.A.F. Mildenhall.

port of Wilhelmshaven. Thus his Command was now fully in the hands of the Admiralty as far as operations were concerned, a somewhat invidious position that would occur again in the coming years, much to the annoyance of other Commanders-in-Chief. In retrospect it might be considered as a blessing in disguise because it actually afforded Bomber Command some breathing space and certainly saved the loss of valuable aircraft and more especially a precious number of trained aircrews. As Air Vice-Marshal Arthur T. Harris, then the A.O.C. of No 5 Group, recalled, 'Any sustained campaign in the autumn of 1939 would very quickly have brought us to the end of our supply of trained crews'.

Of No 3 Group's three operational squadrons in Suffolk, No 149 was still at Mildenhall with No 9 at Honington, but No 99 Squadron had been ordered to make a rapid move to Newmarket Heath and later in the month briefly to Elmdon, Warwickshire. This had been occasioned by the Air Ministry's 'Scatter Plans', a directive that several bomber squadrons should

Blenheim IVs of No 110 Squadron at R.A.F. Wattisham.

be dispersed away from their operational stations in the event of war. It was considered to be a precautionary measure in case of a pre-emptive enemy strike on East Anglian airfields, as had happened in Poland.

Thus, late on 1st September, eleven of No 99's Wellingtons moved onto the racecourse at Newmarket Heath; the Air Ministry had hastily requisitioned a large part of the Rowley Mile, apparently without informing the Clerk of the Course! R.A.F. Newmarket was probably the most unusual bomber station in the whole country and for several years boasted the longest grass runway in Britain. By the outbreak of war the complete Squadron had moved in and although it was originally considered a temporary expedient, the Squadron operated from there until April 1941, but always under the operational control of the parent station.

The two squadrons based at Stradishall – Nos 75 and 215 – had already been allocated to operational training and within a week or so both had moved on, No 75 to Harwell and No 215 to Bramcote, Warwickshire. In any case the airfield had now been placed on 'Care and Maintenance' for the preparation and construction of hard runways. It was not until early 1940 that Stradishall housed its first operational squadron.

No 2 Group had six Blenheim squadrons ready for action, two of which, Nos 107 and 110, formed No 83 Wing at Wattisham. At three minutes past noon on 3rd September a Blenheim IV of No 139 Squadron flown by Flying Officer Andrew McPherson set off from Wyton on the R.A.F.'s first operational sortie of the war, with the objective of making a reconnaissance of the naval port of Wilhelmshaven on the north German coast and to photograph vessels of the German Fleet, which were thought to be leaving the port. The crew sighted a number of warships in the Schillig Roads, which were heading north, but when they arrived back at Wyton some five hours later, there was insufficient time to evaluate the photographs and launch the Command's first bombing raid so the Blenheim crews at Wyton and Wattisham were stood down. However, three Wellington crews of No 149 Squadron were sent out at 16.30 hours but because of the bad weather in the area the crews found it impossible to locate the enemy vessels and they returned safely to Mildenhall five hours later.

The following morning McPherson and his crew were sent out again on a reconnaissance flight of the ports of Wilhelmshaven and Brunsbüttel. The weather was atrocious but the vessels were located. Two of the vessels were thought to be the 'pocket' battleship *Admiral Scheer* and the cruiser *Emden* and as they were anchored well away from the shore they were considered 'legitimate' targets in view of the moratorium about attacking undefended targets. It was decided to launch an immediate attack but with strict orders that 'the greatest care is to be taken not to injure the civilian population. The intention is to destroy the German Fleet. *There is no alternative target*'.

Earlier in the day the Wellington and Blenheim crews placed on standby at Mildenhall, Honington and Wattisham had listened to H.M. King George VI's personal message to the Royal Air Force:

> The Royal Air Force has behind it a tradition no less inspiring than those of the older Services, and in the campaign which we have now been compelled to undertake you will have to assume responsibilities far greater than those which your service had to shoulder in the last war. I can assure all ranks of the air force of my supreme confidence in their skill and courage, and their ability to meet whatever calls may be made upon them.

They were only too aware that in a matter of hours they might well be called upon to assume those 'far greater' responsibilities.

Five Blenheims of No 139 Squadron were the first to leave but they were unable to locate the enemy vessels and so they returned to Wyton. At Wattisham five Blenheims of 'A' Flight of No 110 Squadron led by Flight Lieutenant Kenneth Doran took off, followed about five minutes later by five Blenheims of 'B' Flight of No 107 Squadron. Doran found the vessels by what he later described as 'an incredible combination of luck and judgement' and his crew made the first attack from about 250 ft with three direct hits on the 'pocket' battleship but the 500 lb bombs, which were fitted with eleven-second delay fuses to allow time for the following aircraft to bomb, bounced off the armoured deck and exploded in the sea. One of the following Blenheims was hit by anti-aircraft fire and crashed in flames onto the forecastle of the *Emden,* killing nine Germen seamen and the four-man crew. In a bizarre twist of fate, the pilot, Flying Officer H.L. Emden, died whilst attacking an enemy vessel bearing his surname.

By the time the crews of No 107 Squadron arrived on the scene a few minutes later the anti-aircraft fire from the German vessels was heavy and accurate. Four aircraft were shot down, the last one crashing into the harbour; the three airmen managed to escape from their Blenheim and were rescued by a pilot boat. The pilot, Sergeant A.S. Prince, was mortally wounded and died later in hospital, while Sergeant G.F. Booth and AC1 L.G. Slattery were taken prisoner, the first of over nine thousand, eight hundred Command airmen to become prisoners of war. They remained in captivity until released

---

'The First of the Ten Thousand', a dramatic painting by John Rutherford of the attack on the Admiral Scheer *by a Blenheim of No 107 Squadron, which was piloted by Sergeant A.S. Prince.* (Kind permission of the artist, John Rutherford and the Nanton Lancaster Air Museum, Canada)

Becklingen War Cemetery at Soltau, Germany, where 895 R.A.F. airmen are buried.
(The Commonwealth War Graves Commission)

by the Allied forces in 1945 – the longest spell of captivity suffered by any Allied servicemen; by then both had been promoted to Warrant Officer. The solitary survivor of No 107's Flight only sighted a destroyer and the pilot, Pilot Officer W. Stephens, did not bomb in the hope of sighting the main targets, but in vain, and the crew eventually returned to Wattisham with their bombs.

As one airman at Wattisham recalled.

> There was tremendous excitement when 'A' Flight [110 Squadron] returned and consternation when the lone Blenheim of 107 landed. It occurred to us aircrew that if this was to be the pattern of future operations we were in for a very short career.

Sadly, these words were to prove all too prophetic.

Fourteen Wellingtons from Nos 9 and 149 Squadrons left from Honington and Mildenhall in the mid-afternoon detailed to attack the German Fleet off Brunsbüttel at the entrance to the Kiel Canal. Five of the eight crews of No 149 Squadron aborted the operation because of the atrocious weather conditions; one crew mistook the Elbe river for the Kiel Canal and unfortunately one crew dropped two bombs near Esbjerg in Denmark, about 110 miles north of their target, and two civilians were killed. Two of the six Wellingtons of No 9 Squadron were shot down by what was believed to be anti-aircraft fire but later a pilot of a Messerschmitt Bf 109 claimed one bomber. At the debriefing all the crews told of 'heavy and accurate anti-aircraft fire' as well as 'prolonged and vigorous attacks by enemy fighters'.

Thus ended the Command's first bombing operations of the war; a somewhat inglorious affair and quite frankly it had been a disastrous day. Only thirteen of the twenty-nine crews had found their targets and minimal damage had been sustained by the German vessels – the cruiser *Emden* was put out of action for about two months. Seven aircraft had been lost along with twenty-six airmen, a loss rate of 24%, which could presage a very costly autumn for Bomber Command. The bodies of sixteen airmen were recovered by the German authorities and they were buried with full military honours with a German naval guard of honour at Geestemunde Cemetery. After the war some (including Sergeant A.S. Prince) were removed to Becklingen War Cemetery at Soltau, Germany, where there are the graves of eight hundred and ninety-five R.A.F. airmen. It is just one of nine such War Cemeteries in Germany, the final resting places of so many of the Command's airmen.

The *Daily Mail* headlined the news as 'The First Blow', with the *Daily Telegraph* claiming that 'a successful attack was carried out on vessels of the German fleet'. Flight Lieutenant Doran's interview after the operation was heaven-sent for journalists when he had said that they

> '... could see some washing hanging on the line. Undaunted by the washing we proceeded to bomb the battleship. Flying at 100 ft above mast height all three aircraft in the flight converged on her. I flew straight ahead. The pilot of the second aircraft came across from one side and the third crossed from the other side... We dropped our bombs... and the ship's pom-pom guns began to fire as we headed for home...'

The Ministry of Information declared that 'the Blenheim crews were proud to have been chosen to strike the first blow at the enemy war machine'. What was abundantly clear from this first bombing operation was the unflinching courage with which the attacks were pressed home despite the strong opposition, which became typical of the Command's aircrews throughout the war. On 10th September the first R.A.F. wartime decorations for gallantry were gazetted: Distinguished Flying Crosses to both Flying Officer McPherson and Flight Lieutenant Doran.

These first operations also showed that, as yet, the concept of a dedicated bomber crew had not been realised. Wireless Operators and Air Gunners were skilled ground tradesmen who had volunteered for flying duties on a part-time basis, mainly for the additional flying pay. They had received little formal training for their duties on board and many were of the lowest rank of the Service – Aircraftsman

Distinguished Flying Cross and Distinguished Flying Medal. (Spink & Son Ltd)

Second Class (AC2), more commonly known as an 'Erk'; in fact, ten of the twenty-six airmen missing in action on 4th September were Corporals or below and at least one, AC2 Kenneth G. Day, a gunner in No 9 Squadron, was only twenty years old. In December air gunners were made up to full-time crew members with the rank of Sergeant along with their half-wing 'AG', but nevertheless even as late as mid-June 1940 Corporals, AC1s and AC2s were still flying, and being killed, as air gunners.

Also quite remarkably for this very early stage of the war, the crews engaged on this bombing operation comprised airmen from Britain, Canada, New Zealand, Australia and Eire. This mix of nationalities became a normal feature of Command crews in the years ahead when it was the most cosmopolitan

Sergeant Albert S. Prince of No 107 Squadron, the first Canadian airman to be killed whilst serving in Bomber Command. (Nanton Lancaster Society Air Museum)

force in the Royal Air Force. Sergeant Prince was a Canadian by birth and had joined the R.A.F. in 1935. He was the first of over ten thousand, six hundred and forty Canadians to be killed whilst serving in Bomber Command, the largest number of any Commonwealth country and almost 18% of the Command's total fatalities. On the sixtieth anniversary of his death (4th September 1999) a display in his honour was unveiled at the Nanton Lancaster Air Museum, Alberta, Canada.

Just ten days after these costly operations one of the most charismatic airmen and leaders of the Second World War arrived at Wattisham to take over the command of No 107 Squadron – Wing Commander Basil Embry, D.S.O. He was the epitome of the pre-war Service having joined as a Pilot Officer back in March 1921 and had witnessed all the radical changes in the Service, as well as seeing active service in Iraq and India; just twelve months previously he had been awarded the D.S.O. for operations in Waziristen on the North West Frontier. Before he took over command of the Squadron he had completed just five hours' solo flying in a Blenheim, which was then considered sufficient experience! His first operational sortie took place on 25th September. It was a photo-reconnaissance flight over Münster and although his Blenheim was attacked by two enemy fighters he managed to evade them and returned safely to Wattisham five and a half hours later with just superficial damage to his aircraft. He was greeted by the Station Commander and a senior staff officer from the Group, who immediately fired a stream of questions at him. This taught Embry an important lesson in how to deal with returning crews and he wrote in his book *Mission Completed*:

> They must be not set upon by staff officers and others who had not shared their experiences and be subjected to a barrage of questions, many of which are probably quite irrelevant if put by people untrained in interrogation duties. Immediately after landing, aircrew should be allowed to talk between themselves and exchange experiences, because it is the best way of relieving pent-up feelings and easing off emotional tension built up during a long and difficult mission.

Photo-reconnaissance was now one of the Group's main tasks, as well as searching the North Sea for elements of the German Fleet. Such operations were dangerous, cold and lonely flights but they were undertaken by the crews with great determination and courage. The cameras then used by the R.A.F. were F.24s, which dated back to 1925. Although the F.24 was a most reliable camera, it was not of a very high definition and was not heated,

An F.24 camera being handed to an Observer of a Bristol Blenheim. (R.A.F. Museum)

which caused some technical problems for the crews. The Blenheim was no match for the *Luftwaffe* fighters and flying at a relatively low altitude they became prey to anti-aircraft fire, more commonly known in the Service as 'flak' batteries (the initials of *Flug-Abwehr-Kanone* – German anti-aircraft cannon). From mid-September until late November seven Blenheims were shot down, a loss rate of almost 20%. Two of these came from No 110 Squadron; on 28th September two crews failed to return from flights over Osnabrück, Münster and Kiel – six 'Blenheim Boys' lost in action including

Famous photograph taken by Cecil Beaton of a pilot and co-pilot of a Wellington. The official caption reads: 'Brave yet cautious, cool yet daring'.
(Imperial War Museum)

the Squadron Commander, Wing Commander I. McL. Cameron, another long-serving pre-war officer. Because of the cost in men and machines these flights were abandoned at the end of November.

Despite the experience of the Wellington crews on 4th September, it was still considered that heavy bombers flying in close formation in daylight was more than adequate defence against enemy fighters. The belief that 'the bomber will always get through' was almost a 'sacred cow' in Bomber Command. It was therefore decided that 'as and when necessary armed reconnaissance flights should continue' and to this end No 149 Squadron had been nominated as 'Group Duty Squadron' from 18th September when its crews were placed on a 'two-hour readiness' to take off should the German Fleet set out from their ports.

However, alarm bells should have sounded in Bomber Command Headquarters when, on 29th September, five out of eleven Handley Page Hampdens of No 144 Squadron of No 5 Group were shot down near the island of Heligoland whilst on an 'armed sweep'. It was firmly believed that they had been shot down by anti-aircraft fire rather than enemy fighters but it is now known that they had actually fallen to Bf 109s. Nevertheless No 3 Group Headquarters ordered its squadrons to practise close formation flying, which directly led to a tragic accident over Honington on 30th October when two out of three Wellingtons of No 9 Squadron collided in mid air and crashed in flames; all eleven airmen were killed, including Squadron Leader L.S. Lamb, a New Zealander, who had led a section of the Squadron on 4th September. During October the Wellington squadrons had also been engaged in several fighter affiliation exercises with Hurricanes based at Debden in Essex. At the debriefings the crews expressed the opinion that they had beaten off all the fighter attacks. Any doubts or misgivings about the safety afforded by self-defending formations had thus been quickly dispelled!

During the autumn the seemingly endless 'standbys' and 'stand-downs' for No 149 Squadron's crews at Mildenhall had been alleviated when they were chosen to take part in *The Lion Has Wings*, the first popular wartime film based on the R.A.F. It starred Merle Oberon and Ralph Richardson, as well as the Squadron's airmen, and included live footage of their operation over the Kiel Canal. In November the whole Squadron was marched down to the Comet cinema at Mildenhall to attend the film's premiere. It had been produced by Alexander Korda and the film was quite unashamedly blatant propaganda, with the intention to impress foreign audiences of the potential

A Blenheim pilot ready for a flight over the cold North Sea.
(via M. Harris)

of the R.A.F. Many who saw the film said that it gave them 'a glow of pride' and 'a feeling that all was well in the world'. Quite remarkably, nearly seventy years later the film has been reissued on DVD.

The Wellington crews were back to business in December when, as a result of three operations mounted during the month, Bomber Command's future conduct of the war was effectively and irrevocably changed. The *Official History* later described the operations as 'among the most important of the war'.

On 3rd December Wing Commander R. Kellett of No 149 Squadron led a formation of twenty-four Wellingtons of Nos 149, 38 and 115 Squadrons (the latter were based at Marham, Norfolk) to attack German warships in the Heligoland Bight. Only one crew claimed to have hit a cruiser and enemy fighters, believed to have been alerted by a patrol vessel, attacked the formation, but they were successfully repulsed and a rear gunner of No 38 Squadron, AC1 J. Copley claimed a Bf 109; he was awarded the Distinguished Flying Medal. All the aircraft returned safely and for Command Headquarters this was a further vindication of the efficacy of a self-defending bomber formation.

It was a completely different matter eleven days later (14th) when twelve crews of No 99 Squadron at Newmarket Heath were made ready for another attack in the same area. The Squadron's first operation had taken place a week earlier – reconnaissance and leaflet dropping. But this operation was to be live: each Wellington was loaded with three 500 lb SAP (Semi-Armour Piercing) bombs, with the strict orders to bomb, if possible, from 10,000 ft to achieve maximum penetration, but not lower than 2,000 ft. The formation was led by Acting Wing Commander J.F. Griffiths, who had taken command of the Squadron on 26th September.

During the crossing of the North Sea the weather rapidly and seriously worsened and the formation had to fly at about 300 ft to be below the cloud cover; some of the crew later recalled that it was almost at sea level,

Corporal C.C. Pettitt, D.F.M., Wing Commander J.F. Griffiths, D.F.C. and Corporal A. Bickerstaff of No 99 Squadron at R.A.F. Newmarket Heath. All were awarded gallantry medals for an operation on 14th December 1939. (via M. Harris)

nevertheless their strict close formation was maintained. Enemy vessels were finally sighted but it was impossible to get into a favourable bombing position. The flak they encountered was heavy and the crews came under sustained attacks from enemy fighters; three Wellingtons were shot down and two collided whilst trying to evade the fighters and crashed into the sea but two Messerschmitt Bf 110s were seen to go down in flames. The surviving seven Wellingtons turned for home and one damaged aircraft crash-landed in a field alongside the racecourse, killing three of the crew. Six Wellingtons had been lost along with thirty three airmen, which proved to be the Squadron's heaviest loss on a single operation whilst serving in Bomber Command.

After the debriefings it was still felt that anti-aircraft fire rather than enemy fighters had caused the disaster. Indeed, a Senior Air Staff Officer at Command Headquarters, Air Commodore Norman Bottomley, vouchsafed the opinion:

> It is now by no means certain that enemy fighters did in fact succeed in shooting down any of the Wellingtons... the failure of the enemy must be ascribed to good formation flying. The maintenance of tight, unshaken formations in the face of the most powerful Ironsides. Had it

not been for that good leadership, losses from enemy aircraft might have been heavy.

One can only conjecture what the Air Commodore considered 'heavy losses'! However, Jack Baldwin, the A.O.C. of No 3 Group, held a different view and is reported to have likened the action to that of 'The Charge of the Light Brigade'. Three days later Acting Wing Commander Griffiths was awarded an 'immediate' D.F.C. and Corporals A. Bickerstaff and C.C. Pettitt each the D.F.M. for their destruction of the two fighters. A third was thought to have been brought down but there was insufficient evidence to confirm the victory.

Four days later (18th) twenty-four Wellington crews (nine each from Nos 9 and 149 Squadrons and six from No 37 Squadron at Feltwell, Norfolk) were detailed for another operation over the Heligoland Bight, again led by Wing Commander Kellett. This operation was conducted in clear weather and turned out to be a disaster of some magnitude. Two crews of No 149 Squadron had to abort the operation because of mechanical problems and of the remaining twenty-two no less than ten were shot down by enemy fighters in a ferocious onslaught that lasted about forty minutes. The *Luftwaffe* had received an early warning of their approach from the experimental *Freya* RDF (Radar) station on the island of Wangerooge. But it was No 37 Squadron bringing up the rear that suffered the heaviest loss: five out of six crews. No 9 Squadron lost four aircraft in action and a fifth was so heavily damaged that it crashed into the sea off Cromer; five of the crew were rescued by a trawler, one of the gunners had been killed in action. Another gunner, AC1 C.R. Driver, was awarded the D.F.M. for his brave actions during the operation and at the age of eighteen years he was then the youngest airman to be awarded a gallantry medal. A Wellington of No 149 Squadron was the first to fall to the enemy fighters but a second aircraft crashed into the sea about sixty miles from the Norfolk coast; none of the crew were rescued.

Wing Commander Kellett was awarded the D.F.C. for his leadership of this ill-fated operation. This was the second operation within ten days with a 50% loss rate – twelve aircraft lost, and sixty-one airmen missing in action of whom only five survived as prisoners of war. Perhaps it was not too surprising that this area around Heligoland, Brunsbüttel and Wilhelmshaven became known to the crews as the 'Hornets' Nest'!

There seemed to be no doubt now that the cherished concept of a self-defending bomber formation was seriously flawed. Nevertheless, it was still felt in Command Headquarters that poor formation flying had been a contributory

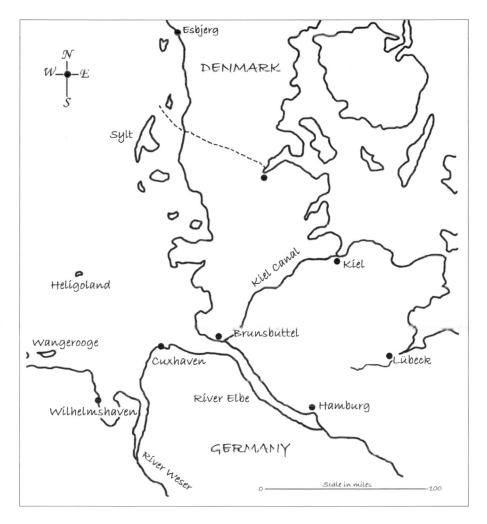

Map of the 'Hornets' Nest'; the area where Bomber Command's first operations were conducted.

cause and the relatively light losses suffered by the tight formation held by No 149 Squadron under Kellett's close leadership was cited as an example. These two costly operations did not suddenly change the Command's mode of operations but rather brought about a postponement. There were other pressing problems to address. Firstly, the Wellingtons 'seemed to burn very easily', thus the provision of seal-sealing fuel tanks was an urgent matter, as

A close formation of No 9 Squadron's Wellingtons: the theory of a self-defending formation for daylight operations was seriously flawed. (R.A.F. Museum)

indeed was the strengthening of the aircraft armament. Air Chief Marshal Sir Edgar Ludlow-Hewitt had long harboured doubts about the proficiency of air gunners, which were only heightened by these two operations. The severe weather during the winter of 1939/40 allowed some precious time for a radical reappraisal of the way forward for Bomber Command.

In these first months of the air war Bomber Command had been taught a few harsh and costly lessons. When they counted the cost of their operations by the four Groups, over ninety aircraft had been lost in action and training accidents; but this was not a serious problem as sufficient replacement aircraft were now readily available. The deeper concern for the Command's chiefs was the loss of over two hundred and twenty trained airmen, many of whom were 'the cream' of the pre-war Service, known as the 'true blues'. Although this period of the war (and up to April 1940) was dubbed the 'Phoney War', it was certainly anything but for Bomber Command and its brave crews.

The crews flying from the four Suffolk airfields had borne the brunt of those 'harsh and costly lessons'. When a Blenheim IV of No 107 Squadron was lost on 27th December whilst on a reconnaissance flight over the dreaded Schillig Roads, the total number of aircraft lost in action by the Suffolk squadrons totalled thirty-five (twenty-five Wellingtons and ten Blenheims) and another six aircraft had been lost in training accidents; tragically, one hundred and twenty-four airmen had been killed. Unfortunately the situation would only worsen in 1940, especially for the 'Blenheim Boys' at Wattisham.

Chapter 3

A Fateful Year

(1940)

In many respects 1940 proved to be a critical year for Bomber Command and its crews and, perhaps with the benefit of hindsight, it might be considered the most fateful one of the Command's long war. During 1940 it had no less than three different Commanders-in-Chief, as well as several Command changes at Group level. But the most notable feature was the abandonment of daylight operations by heavy bombers and their wholehearted commitment to night bombing.

The year saw the start of the Command's strategic bombing offensive against German industries, the bombing of the 'ultimate' target, Berlin, and for the first time over one hundred heavy bombers being sent out on a single night, as well as the crews' first mine-laying operations, which continued and increased in volume almost to the end of the war. The operational training of crews was placed on a much more efficient and effective basis with the formation of the first Operational Training Units. Towards the end of 1940 the first operation was directed on the centre of a German city, later known as 'area bombing'. These important milestones really formed the basis of the Command's bombing offensive for the rest of the war.

Despite the heavy losses suffered in December 1939, further attempts were made to locate and bomb German warships in the North Sea. These daylight operations were mainly undertaken by the Wellington and Blenheim crews. During the first ten days of January, No 149 Squadron lost two Wellingtons whilst on a reconnaissance flight and twelve airmen were killed, half of them of the rank of LAC or below. Eight days later, a Blenheim of No 110 Squadron was shot down by Bf 110s over the North Sea and another two

A winter scene at R.A.F. Newmarket Heath – Wellington of No 99 Squadron protected against the severe weather. (via R. Roberts)

were 'written-off' with severe battle damage.

Late in January Air Chief Marshal Sir Edgar Ludlow-Hewitt warned the Air Ministry that there was 'the urgent necessity to reconsider the whole question of daylight operations ... and to study the possibility of devising some other means of employing the bomber striking force to the best effect ...'. Nevertheless, the conversion of Bomber Command to a predominantly night force was still several months away.

The severe weather – long spells of intense cold and heavy snowfalls – from late January right into March greatly restricted operations both by day and night. When conditions allowed, the Wellington crews were engaged on 'Nickel' operations, the dropping of propaganda leaflets over Germany by night or what the crews referred to as 'confetti throwing'! It was estimated that over 1,500 *million* leaflets were delivered throughout the course of the war. The value of these 'Nickel' operations has long been debated considering the number of airmen that were killed; they were once described as 'a monstrously ineffective means to a useless end'! However, the Air Ministry considered them an essential part of the psychological war and furthermore they provided valuable night flying and navigation experience for the crews.

The so-called 'Phoney War' came to an abrupt end in early April when German forces invaded Denmark and Norway on the 9th and, for the next month, the Command crews were engaged in attacking airfields in Norway and Denmark and enemy shipping along the coasts. During this time No 149 Squadron lost three Wellington crews and No 99 Squadron suffered two crews missing in action. The two Blenheim squadrons, Nos 107 and 110, operated in turn from Lossiemouth in northeast Scotland, from where they lost six crews.

On 12th April the Wellington crews of Nos 149 and 99 Squadrons were engaged on what proved to be the last major daylight operation for Bomber Command heavy bombers for the next four years. Out of the sixty engaged over Stavanger airfield, nine were lost (15%) to heavy flak and enemy fighters. Amongst the two crews of No 149's Wellingtons killed in action

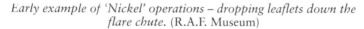

Early example of 'Nickel' operations – dropping leaflets down the flare chute. (R.A.F. Museum)

Loading 250 lb bombs into a Blenheim IV.

*Bombing up a Wellington – 'OJ-N Firefly' – of No 149 Squadron at Mons Wood,
Mildenhall.* (Imperial War Museum)

was Corporal J.H. Langridge, R.N.Z.A.F., who was thought to be the first of some one thousand, six hundred and seventy New Zealanders to be killed whilst serving with Bomber Command. Then, on the night of 17/18th, a Wellington of No 99 Squadron failed to return from the same target. The pilot, Flying Officer A.F. Smith, was a South African serving with the R.A.F.; twenty-four members of the S.A.A.F. would subsequently lose their lives whilst serving in the Command; further evidence of its strong international make-up. His co-pilot, Pilot Officer John G.C. Salmond, was the son of Air Chief Marshal Sir Geoffrey Salmond. He was only twenty years old. The Salmond family was one of the most illustrious in the Service; Geoffrey's brother, John, had also attained the rank of Chief of the Air Staff. The six-man crew have no known graves and their names appear on the R.A.F. Memorial at Runnymede. Their average age was twenty-one years, which was quite unusual at this stage of the war when so many pre-war airmen were serving in the Command.

The Norwegian campaign claimed another celebrated pilot and leader, Squadron Leader Kenneth Doran, D.F.C., Bar, who had led the Blenheims on 4th September 1939. His Blenheim was shot down by enemy fighters on the 30th whilst over Norway; he survived as a prisoner of war but the other two airmen were killed.

The change to night bombing was a momentous decision for Bomber Command and its crews; henceforth the majority of the many thousands of airmen that served in Bomber Command would only operate by night. Perhaps it was sheer coincidence that just a week earlier (3rd), Air Marshal Sir Charles 'Peter' Portal had been appointed A.O.C.-in-Chief of Bomber Command replacing Air Chief Marshal Sir Edgar Ludlow-Hewitt, who was appointed the Inspector-General of the R.A.F., a post he held until 1945. Also during the month a new Commander arrived at No 2 Group, Air Vice-Marshal James N. Robb, D.S.O., D.F.C., both awards having been made during the First World War when he had been a successful fighter pilot. He was destined to command the Group during its greatest ordeal, a time when a posting to the Group was likened to 'a sentence of death'.

Early on 10th May German troops invaded Belgium and Holland and the seven Blenheim squadrons were placed on 'immediate readiness'. Over the next six weeks the Blenheim crews flew over fifteen hundred sorties and eighty aircraft were lost in action along with two hundred and forty-six airmen; no other R.A.F. Group suffered such heavy losses in a relatively brief period. As Michael Bowyer commented in his admirable history of No

2 Group: 'its costly contribution to the Battle of France was nothing short of heroic, every man who participated was a hero'.

The Group's role in the Battle for France had already been clearly defined: 'To locate the advance of the enemy's columns, attack armed fighting vehicles, bomb captured airfields in Holland and Belgium and to destroy road and rail bridges in front of the enemy's advance'. The crews would be operating at low level over or near the battlefield, where the German fighters and the mobile flak batteries were present in strength. It was perhaps not too surprising that the Blenheim crews, along with the ill-fated Fairey Battle crews of the Advanced Air Striking Force, suffered horrendous losses in a most courageous but ultimately futile attempt to stem the enemy's inexorable advance.

From 10th May until the end of June the Blenheim crews were in action daily, and on some days two operations were flown; as Sir Basil Embry later recalled, 'by the law of averages one's survival was impossible'.

Bridges across the River Meuse; during May 1940 many Blenheim crews were lost attacking bridges.

Wellington crews prepare for an operation – fleece-lined jackets, flying rations, a thermos of soup or coffee and a parachute.

He also maintained that no aircraft returned without extensive battle damage. During this period the two Wattisham squadrons lost thirty-four Blenheims, with fifty airmen missing in action, only ten of whom survived as prisoners of war. Compared with the overall losses of the Group when some squadrons were virtually decimated, it might be said that both Nos 107 and 110 Squadrons escaped the mayhem relatively lightly, though I do stress *relatively*, as these overall figures mask two disastrous days for the squadrons. On 12th May, No 107 lost four out of its twelve crews sent to bomb the bridges at Maastricht; one of the airmen killed on this operation was AC2 J.R. Mayor, whose award of the D.F.M. had only been gazetted

Recruitment Office. During and after the Battle of Britain many young men volunteered for the R.A.F.; there was never a shortage of volunteers.

five days earlier. Two days later No 107 Squadron lost five crews out of twelve whilst attacking the River Meuse crossing point at Sedan.

The worst day to befall the Squadron and Wattisham was 27th May, when Wing Commander Basil Embry was posted missing in action along with another crew whilst attacking enemy columns concentrated at St Omer. Shortly before the operation Embry had been informed that he was to take over command of R.A.F. West Raynham, Norfolk, at the rank of acting Group Captain. He was so keen to remain with his squadron during this difficult period that he tried unsuccessfully to postpone the posting, although his replacement, Wing Commander L.G. Stokes, was already at Wattisham.

Embry led twelve Blenheims in his final operation from Wattisham; his replacement was also engaged in the operation. Embry's Blenheim was shot down by heavy flak in the target area and he and Pilot Officer T.A. Whiting baled out; his gunner, Corporal G.E. Long, had already been killed. Embry's truly remarkable escape from captivity is related in his book *Mission Completed*. He escaped twice from prison and made it on foot, by cycle and other transport down through France, across the Pyrenees and through Spain to Gibraltar. This was at a time when the celebrated 'escape lines' had yet to be established. He finally reached Plymouth on 2nd August and returned to Wattisham exactly nine weeks and five days after being

Wing Commander Basil Embry, D.S.O., took over the command of No 107 Squadron. He was one of the outstanding airmen and leaders of the Second World War. (R.A.F. Museum)

shot down; a third bar was added to his D.S.O. Embry ultimately returned to No 2 Group as its last wartime Commander shortly before it was transferred into the 2nd Tactical Air Force in late May 1943. He ranks alongside such names as Douglas Bader, Percy Pickard, Guy Gibson and Leonard Cheshire as one of the outstanding airmen and leaders of the Second World War. He retired from the R.A.F. in 1956 and died in 1977 aged seventy-five years.

During those early summer months the chances of survival as a 'Blenheim Boy' were very slim indeed – as Air Marshal Portal famously commented, '... [they] were being lost at a rate of one or two squadrons per week ...'. Amongst those fortunate to survive was Flight Lieutenant Harold P. 'Flash' Pleasance, also of No 107 Squadron. He flew on Embry's last operation

Wellingtons of No 214 Squadron at R.A.F. Stradishall in 1940. They arrived in June. (Imperial War Museum)

Flight Lieutenant Harold 'Flash' Pleasance of No 107 Squadron was one of the 'Blenheim Boys' who survived the horrendous losses of 1940.

and later recalled, 'I must be one of the very few who saw one Squadron Commander hand over command to his successor in the air!'. On 7th June Pleasance was awarded an immediate D.F.C. for 'displaying great gallantry and deep devotion to duty' for a lone reconnaissance flight to locate enemy forces crossing the Somme. He had been injured in the leg and was forced to land his damaged aircraft in France. After receiving emergency medical attention he and his crew later returned to Wattisham. On 10th July he led six Blenheims of No 107 Squadron to bomb an airfield at Amiens. They encountered heavy and intense flak and he and his crew were the only ones to survive, nine airmen killed and six taken prisoner of war. One of these, Sergeant C.G. Hoskins, was killed on 19th April 1945 when a marching

column of prisoners of war was fired upon by Allied aircraft, how tragic after spending almost five years in captivity and so near the end of the war in Europe. In January 1941 Pleasance joined his old Squadron Commander, Embry, at R.A.F. Wittering where he became a successful night fighter pilot flying Bristol Beaufighters. He retired from the R.A.F. in 1960 as a Group Captain with the O.B.E., D.F.C., Bar and MiD (Mentioned in Despatches) to his name; he died in June 2004 aged ninety years.

During May the air war changed quite dramatically for the heavy bomber squadrons when on the 15th the *Luftwaffe* bombed Rotterdam and almost one thousand Dutch civilians were killed; the War Cabinet immediately authorised Bomber Command to cross the Rhine to bomb German industrial targets. Thus, on the night of 15/16th May, ninety-nine heavy bombers were sent out to sixteen industrial targets and all returned safely; the Command's strategic bombing offensive had begun. From now on, in between operations in support of the beleaguered British ground troops at Dunkirk, the Wellington crews were mainly engaged over Germany with the three Suffolk squadrons - Nos 9, 99 and 149 - sustaining light losses. Many crews returned to report that although the flak opposition was heavy they had barely seen an enemy night fighter.

In June another Wellington squadron entered the fray. Earlier in the year (February) Stradishall, now resplendent with its three firm runways each about 1,000 yards long, became an active operational station in No 3 Group when No 214 Squadron arrived from Methwold, Norfolk. The Squadron had been formed back in July 1917 as a heavy night bombing unit, hence its motto, *Ulltor in umbris* or 'Avenging in the shadows'. It had reformed in 1935 and received its Wellingtons back in May 1939. In 1941 it became known as 'Federated Malay States' having been adopted by that Federation. The Squadron was destined to serve at three Suffolk airfields until December 1943.

Its first operation was mounted on 14/15th June when two crews were sent out on a 'Razzle' operation over southern Germany. These were effectively 'fire-raising' missions and were among the more hare-brained schemes devised in the pre-war days. It was thought that starting fires in the Black Forest and making incendiary attacks on the German harvest would greatly lower the morale of the German people! These forms of attacks continued well into September but are now considered to have been a considerable waste of time and resources.

One of these operations led indirectly to the first successful escape from a P.O.W. camp by a R.A.F. officer. On 5/6th September a Wellington of No 149 Squadron was shot down whilst on a 'Razzle' operation to the Black Forest; all the airmen were taken prisoner and the pilot, Flying Officer Harold 'Harry' Burton, was taken to *Stalag Luft I* at Barth on the Baltic coast. On 27th May 1941 he successfully tunnelled his way out and made it to a nearby ferry-port, Stralsund. He secreted himself under a lorry which was being loaded on the ferry for Sweden. After a short period of internment in Sweden he arrived back in Britain in July and was awarded the D.S.O. Burton toured stations to give lectures and advice to crews on his experiences whilst on the run in Germany. He retired from the R.A.F. in 1973 as an Air Chief Marshal.

During June, targets in northern Italy were attacked for the first time shortly after Italy had entered the war. Crews of Nos 99 and 149 Squadrons were despatched to a landing ground at Salon-en-Provence in southern France to launch attacks on Genoa and Milan. After some high-level political debate the French government finally granted permission and on two successive nights from 15th to 17th the Wellington crews were in action over the two Italian cities; but they encountered severe storms and few of them were able to bomb. On 17th June the French government surrendered and the crews were hastily recalled but with strict orders to destroy any aircraft that could not be flown back; two of No 99's Wellingtons suffered this fate. Also during the month, No 218 Squadron arrived at Mildenhall from France with its Fairey Battles, but it was only a brief stay as it moved away to Oakington, Cambridgeshire where it would be re-equipped with Blenheims.

After the fall of France No 2 Group was issued with an order: 'It is essential that the destructive effects of our night bombing operations over Germany should be continued throughout daylight by sporadic attacks on the same objectives. The intention is to make attacks only when cloud cover gives adequate security. These attacks will be made *regardless of cost* [my italics]'. Each Blenheim Wing was allocated separate targets; the Wattisham squadrons were allotted the oil refineries at Hamburg and Wanne-Eickel along with the marshalling yards at Hamm and Osnabrück. The Blenheim crews were also engaged in attacking enemy airfields as well as ports in Holland, Belgium and Northern France where a large armada of sea-going barges was being assembled for the proposed invasion of Britain. Many of these operations were conducted at night although the Blenheims were not properly equipped for night operations, nor indeed had their crews much practical experience of night flying. Their contribution to the Battle of Britain was acknowledged by Winston Churchill in his famous speech of 26th August:

> On no part of the R.A.F. does the weight of the war fall more heavily than on the daylight bombers, who play an invaluable part in the case of an invasion and whose unfailing zeal it has been necessary in the meantime on numerous occasions to restrain.

Certainly, during and after the Battle of Britain many young men volunteered for the R.A.F. and there was never a shortage of volunteers for flying duties. However, there was a dearth of experienced pilots as it then took almost twelve months to train a bomber pilot up to an operational level.

During July and August the Command's offensive against German targets began to gain some pace and momentum. On 25/26th July it launched its largest operation of the war so far; one hundred and sixty-two aircraft were sent to seven Ruhr targets and enemy airfields in Holland, of which six were lost including a Wellington of No 99 Squadron, which was shot down by a Bf110 over Dortmund. The captain, Pilot Officer B.A. Power, and the front gunner, Sergeant K.R. Selwood were killed but the other four crew members baled out and survived as prisoners of war. There

Flight Lieutenant Jens Henning 'Morian' Hansen, D.F.C., G.C., at the end of the war. (The Royal Danish Library)

was some slight satisfaction when minutes later a gunner in another of the Squadron's Wellingtons, Pilot Officer Jens H.F. 'Morian' Hansen, shot down the fighter. He was the first air gunner of a heavy bomber to destroy a night fighter and was awarded an immediate D.F.C. Hansen was of Danish birth and had been a celebrated pre-war speedway rider, known as the 'Great Dane'. He had settled in England and had gained his flying certificate in 1935. Hansen had volunteered for the R.A.F in 1939 but at the age of thirty-three years he was considered to be too old for pilot duties so was trained as an air gunner. On 18th December he was awarded an honorary George Cross for 'conspicuous heroism' in saving two airmen from a blazing Wellington that had crashed into Devil's Dyke near the airfield at Newmarket. Hansen survived the war as a Flight Lieutenant; in 1984 Danish television celebrated his remarkable life with a *This is Your Life* programme in his honour. He died in 1995 at the age of ninety years.

In July, quite remarkably, another member of No 107 Squadron, Sergeant Robert Lonsdale, repeated Basil Embry's feat of escaping captivity and evading recapture. He was the observer in a Blenheim IV shot down whilst attacking an airfield at Amiens on his fourth operation. Although he and the other survivor, Sergeant B. George, managed to evade capture for several days, Lonsdale was finally captured by the Germans, but whilst being transported to another prison he escaped. After many adventures Lonsdale finally arrived in Gibraltar on 11th April 1941 and for whatever reason he was not awarded a Military Medal until March 1942. Lonsdale was later commissioned and after completing a total of forty-nine operations he was awarded the D.F.C. By a strange coincidence his Group Commander at that time was none other than Air Vice-Marshal Basil Embry!

In late August (25/26th) Berlin was bombed for the first time by way of reprisal for the *Luftwaffe*'s attack on London on the previous night. It is thought that just fewer than fifty Wellingtons and Hampdens attacked the city, but it was anything but successful as heavy cloud greatly hampered the bombing with most of the bombs falling in the countryside to the south of Berlin. Six Hampdens were lost but the British press greeted the news with reports of 'Great Fires in Berlin'. The crews that returned safely to their airfields were jubilant; to have bombed the 'Big B' and survived was very satisfying. Throughout the war all the crews wanted to have Berlin in their logbooks. In the months ahead Berlin became almost a routine target for the heavy bomber crews. On 23rd/24th September, when the city was the target for 129 crews, which was the largest operation so far, quite remarkably only three aircraft were lost; but Nos 9 and 214 Squadrons each lost a crew on this night.

In the last three months of the year the Wellington crews were engaged over a variety of targets in the Ruhr as well as Hamburg, Berlin and Mannheim. It was during this period (5th October) that the third Commander-in-Chief – Air Marshal Sir Richard Peirse – was appointed and Sir Charles Portal was made Chief of the Air Staff. As such he remained a strong and influential voice and presence on the Command's progress and offensive throughout the war.

Two fatal incidents during November graphically illustrated the need for crews to remain vigilant right until the moment that they had landed safely. On 5/6th a crew of No 214 Squadron was returning from Hamburg and whilst they were approaching Stradishall to land another Wellington cut across their flight path, which caused the pilot, Sergeant G. F. Turner, to lose control of the aircraft which crashed only a mile from the airfield with a total loss of life. The following night a Wellington of No 99 Squadron was returning from the Ruhr when it was thought to have been shot down only 150 yards from the Suffolk coast, again with a total loss of life. To have survived enemy flak and night fighters only to crash within sight of England or near the safety of their airfield seemed to be particularly harsh and even more tragic.

On 16/17th December the Wellington crews were in action over Mannheim; the operation was codenamed *Abigail Rachel* and it was directed at the

A Blenheim crew 'studying a map before a raid', according to the official caption.

centre of the city. It had been approved by the War Cabinet in retaliation
for the *Luftwaffe*'s heavy raids on Coventry and Southampton. A handful of
experienced Wellington crews were first over the target and dropped solely
incendiaries with the intention of setting off fires to guide the Main Force
onto the target. Of the one hundred and thirty-four crews taking part almost
80% claimed to have bombed, but although visibility was good – there was
a full moon – the bombing was not particularly accurate. Fortunately the
anti-aircraft fire was light and only three aircraft were lost in action, but
another five crashed on return to England, including a Wellington of No 149
Squadron near Mildenhall and one from No 99 Squadron at Rye, Sussex

but thankfully with no loss of life. This operation highlighted many of the problems that the Command would have to address in the next eighteen months or so – night navigation, target marking and accurate bombing in all weather conditions and more especially over the targets in the Ruhr where heavy industrial haze and intense flak exacerbated such problems, as indeed did the burgeoning of the *Luftwaffe*'s night fighter force.

As the first complete year of the war came to an end, the Command was really not much stronger than it had been back in January. It had been a long and hard twelve months, during which time over seven hundred and sixty aircraft had been lost in action and over two thousand, four hundred and fifty airmen were missing in action; the majority of these were Sergeants, many of whom had entered via the Volunteer Reserve. The Suffolk squadrons had suffered more than their fair share of these losses: seventy-seven Blenheims and seventy-four Wellingtons lost in action along with over three hundred and twenty airmen killed and another eighty-five taken prisoner of war, which amounted to one-fifth of the Command's totals casualties. One of these prisoners of war was Flight Lieutenant E.S. 'Hank' Humphreys of No 107 Squadron, whose Blenheim was shot down over Lannion airfield on 19/20th December. He participated in the celebrated 'Great Escape' from *Stalag Luft III* in March 1944 but was subsequently captured and was one of the fifty escapees that were executed by the Gestapo. As has already been noted, not all prisoners survived the war.

Chapter 4

'Nothing Without Labour'

(1941)

The year 1941 proved to be a most difficult one for Bomber Command; indeed as the year came to a close its very future would be in doubt. The Blenheim squadrons, after their heavy losses in 1940, fared little better, especially during the summer months. In the New Year the crews found themselves engaged in a new type of operation: 'Circus'. These daylight missions involved maybe a handful of crews, escorted by a large number of fighters, being despatched to Belgium, Holland and northern France. Their targets were generally fairly insignificant because the main object was to draw the *Luftwaffe* into the air to occupy them and prevent them being moved to the Russian Front. The operations were not particularly successful and, furthermore, they were limited by the operational range of their escorts. Although losses were relatively light the crews disliked these operations as they felt, with some justification, that they were being used as 'live bait'.

The Wellington crews of No 3 Group also had a trying time, its motto – *Niet Zonder Arbyt* or 'Nothing Without Labour' – proving to be most fitting for its operations during 1941. The Group suffered the heaviest losses of the four heavy bomber groups; three hundred and eighty-two aircraft lost in action. During the year a number of directives were issued, which frequently changed the Command's priorities for its planned campaign – the heavy bombing of Germany's industrial might. Perhaps the most notable diversion

No 3 Group's badge – its motto Niet Zonder Arbyt *means 'Nothing Without Labour'.*

was the number of times that the crews were called upon to attack the German Fleet vessels *Scharnhorst*, *Gneisenau* and *Prinz Eugen*, whilst they sheltered in the French Atlantic ports. Also as a result of the critical nature of the 'Battle of the Atlantic', U-boat ports and yards – Kiel, Hamburg, Bremen and Vegesack – were attacked on numerous occasions, along with their bases at Lorient, Brest and St Nazaire. But, on 15th January, Air Marshal Peirse was instructed that 'the sole and primary aim of your bomber offensive should be the destruction of the German synthetic oil plants'; seventeen targets were specifically listed, names that would figure large in the Command's offensive over the next three years.

It was also a year of change at the Suffolk airfields. In March the control of Newmarket Heath was transferred to Stradishall and the Headquarters of No 3 Group moved out of Mildenhall and relocated to Harraton House at Exning, near Newmarket. Early in March No 107 Squadron left for Leuchars in Scotland and did not return to Wattisham. It was not replaced until late May when No 226 Squadron arrived from Northern Ireland. Also in the month No 99 Squadron moved from Newmarket Heath to a new airfield at Waterbeach in Cambridgeshire after nearly nine years of service in Suffolk. But the most important change for the 'Blenheim Boys' was the appointment in February of a new Commander – Air Vice-Marshal Donald Stevenson, D.S.O., M.C. and Bar. He proved to be a severe and uncompromising

The rather informal briefing of crews in 1941. Briefings soon became much more formal affairs. (via J. Adams)

Crews of No 149 Squadron walking out to their Wellingtons at R.A.F. Mildenhall. (via D.M. Gower)

Commander, who became most unpopular with his crews; they felt that he placed his own career prospects ahead of any concern for his airmen. Stevenson followed his orders to the extreme and the heavy losses sustained during his ten months of tenure earned him the nickname 'Red Steve'! On 17th December he was replaced by Air Vice-Marshal Alan Lees, D.S.O., A.F.C.

Considering all the problems that Bomber Command encountered later in the year, the New Year started in a most promising and aggressive manner when, on 1st/2nd January, over one hundred and forty aircraft bombed Bremen, followed by attacks on the same target on two successive nights. These raids were believed to have caused heavy damage; returning crews reported numerous large fires especially at the Focke-Wulf aircraft factories. On 4/5th Brest was bombed 'more than effectively' according to Command Headquarters, who were also pleased to report that out of the three hundred and twelve aircraft engaged on these four nights only two were lost in action, although four crashed on return to England. Sadly these operations gave a false impression, not only of the effectiveness of the bombing but also the losses of aircraft and airmen.

Because of the severe weather conditions the Command's operations were greatly restricted until the end of February, but from then on its offensive began to gain momentum, although in March the crews were stood down for a whole week because of the weather. Nevertheless Cologne, Dusseldorf, Bremen, Berlin, Brest, Hamburg, Gelsenkirchen and Lorient were attacked, some on several nights, and the losses slowly started to increase with each of the three Suffolk squadrons, Nos 9, 149 and 214, losing crews in action. A Wellington of No 149 Squadron was preparing to land after a raid on Bremen on 17/18th March when the aircraft was shot down by an enemy intruder – a Junkers Ju 88C of NJG2. The Wellington crashed onto a cottage at Beck Row and the six airmen (all Sergeants) were killed; all-Sergeant crews were now becoming far more prevalent. These German intruders were very active in the East Anglian night skies especially during the summer, but perhaps more so over Cambridgeshire and Norfolk; they were a further hazard for the exhausted crews to face when they were so close to the safety of their home airfield. Six months later a Wellington of No 99 Squadron returning from Cologne and which had been diverted to land at Mildenhall, suffered the same fate and also crashed at Beck Row with just the rear gunner escaping unharmed.

Whilst on an operation to Cologne on 27/28th March a Wellington of No 9 Squadron piloted by Flight Lieutenant J.T.L. Shore was shot down by a night fighter over Belgium. He and his crew managed to bale out and were taken prisoner. Shore and his co-pilot, Pilot Officer J.L.R. Long, were taken to *Stalag Luft I*, at Barth on the Baltic coast. Shore, along with another celebrated escapee, Pilot Officer B.A. 'Jimmy' James, managed to tunnel out, and although James was recaptured, John Shore made his way to the nearby Rügen Island and from its port of Saasnitz, he boarded a ferry to Sweden, where he was interned and finally released in the autumn. On his return to Britain he was awarded the Military Cross. Shore was then only the second R.A.F. airman to escape from a prisoner of war camp. He survived the war as a Wing Commander but died in post-war service whilst flying an Avro Lincoln. Sadly, Pilot Officer 'Cookie' Long (his nickname was derived from his skill in distilling alcohol whilst in captivity!) did not survive the war. He was involved in the 'Great Escape' from *Stalag Luft III* in March 1944 and when recaptured he was executed by the Gestapo – the second airman from a Suffolk airfield to be so callously murdered. By a strange coincidence, 'Jimmy' James also took part in the 'Great Escape' but when recaptured he was sent to a concentration camp and survived.

Early in March No 149 Squadron received its first Wellington IIs, which were equipped with more powerful Merlin X engines and had been specially adapted to carry the new 4,000 lb H.C. (High Capacity) bombs, known to the crews as 'Cookies' and to the Germans as *Luftminen*. The new bomb was used in operations for the first time on 31st March/1st April when two Wellington crews were detailed to bomb Emden; one, OJ-G *Wizard of Oz*, failed to get airborne but the other Wellington II along with one from No 9 Squadron were successful. The 'Cookie' became the standard bomb for the Command over the next few years.

There were not that many of the Command's airmen, like John Shore,

J.R. 'Benny' Goodman (second on the left) as a young Sergeant pilot with No 99 Squadron. (via R. Roberts)

who served in these early years and yet still managed to survive the war. Nevertheless, there were at least three such airmen serving with Suffolk squadrons at the time, all of whom went on to have illustrious wartime careers. One of No 99 Squadron's young Sergeant pilots – the nineteen-year-old J.R. 'Benny' Goodman – had started his operational life with No 37 Squadron at Feltwell in May 1940 but moved to No 99 Squadron in November. Goodman completed his first tour with the Squadron in April 1942 and later served as a Mosquito pilot with both Nos 109 and 627 Squadrons in the celebrated Pathfinder Force. He finally completed seventy-nine wartime operations and retired from the R.A.F. as a Group Captain D.F.C., Bar, A.F.C. The Air Force Cross had been instituted in 1918 and usually denoted fine flying skills; it was awarded for 'devotion to flying duties' other than in operations against the enemy. In retirement Goodman became a most active President of No 99 Squadron Association. He died in August 2007 aged eighty-five years.

Squadron Leader H.E. 'Hal' Bufton, one of No 9 Squadron's Flight

Commanders, achieved a most remarkable war service. He was probably the epitome of the pre-war R.A.F. officer; a product of the Service's College at Cranwell and commissioned in 1936. During 1940, whilst he was serving in the highly secret Blind Approach Technical Development Unit, he was credited with discovering the technical details of *Knickebein*, the *Luftwaffe's* radio beam navigational aid. In early 1941 he was posted to No 9 Squadron and on 26/27th August whilst on a raid to Cologne his Wellington was shot

Group Captain H.E. 'Hal' Bufton, D.S.O., O.B.E., D.F.C., A.F.C. (R.A.F. Museum)

down; three of his crew were captured but he and another two crew members evaded capture and they finally returned to Britain by Christmas 1941. In July 1942 he returned briefly to Suffolk when he was promoted to Wing Commander and given the command of No 109 Squadron, which pioneered the use of *Oboe*, the radar blind-bombing device, in the Command's operations. The Squadron operated from Stradishall from early April to early August. At the end of the war Hal Bufton was a Group Captain in charge of R.A.F. Bourn in Cambridgeshire, with the D.S.O., O.B.E., D.F.C. and A.F.C. to his name. He retired from the R.A.F. in 1961 and died in Canada in 1972 at the age of fifty-six.

The third airman, Warrant Officer J.G. 'Roy' Ralston, was a 'Blenheim Boy' and a 'Trenchard Brat' and/or a 'Halton Brat'; this was the nickname given to those airmen who had been trained at the Aircraft Apprentice School at Halton. Roy Ralston was just one of hundreds of 'Trenchard Brats' that served with great distinction in Bomber Command during the war. He had entered Halton at the age of fifteen years and by December 1937 he was

J.'Roy' Ralston, D.S.O., Bar, A.F.C., D.F.M., as a Group Captain towards the end of the war.

a Sergeant pilot; in August 1940 he was posted to No 107 Squadron at Wattisham and survived despite all the heavy losses of those times. He was commissioned in December 1941 and later became a Mosquito pilot *par excellence*, serving in the Pathfinder Force, both operationally and at its Headquarters. In 1945 he was a Wing Commander in command of No 139 (P.F.F.) Squadron, having completed ninety-one operations and been awarded the D.S.O., Bar, A.F.C. and D.F.M.

Ralston and his fellow 'Blenheim Boys' experienced a most torrid time when the ill-fated and very costly 'Channel Stop' operations started in April. The objective of these daylight operations was 'to prevent any enemy vessel to pass through the English Channel from Cherbourg to Ostend'. It was really quite an unrealistic demand considering the resources of the Group at that time – seven Blenheim squadrons totalling about one hundred and thirty-five aircraft, which was almost the same number that were lost in these operations over the next six months.

For 'Channel Stop' each Blenheim squadron was detached in rotation to Manston in Kent, where it was said that 'its average life was about two weeks by which time it was depleted to such an extent that it had to be replaced or withdrawn'. The Blenheim crews usually went out in pairs escorted by fighters and the shipping attacks involved a slow dive from about 5,000 ft to a low-level attack on the vessel through heavy anti-aircraft fire. Many of the missing Blenheims crashed into the sea, or onto or near the enemy vessel. Although No 110 Squadron spent almost six months away from Wattisham in a variety of detachments, including a month in Malta, it lost five crews in these operations, including Flight Lieutenant G. Links and his crew on

A Blenheim IV attacking enemy shipping.

26th April. He had taken part in the famous raid on Wilhelmshaven on 4th September 1939 and his two colleagues were 'veterans' of the summer of 1940; all were killed. On 6th May the Squadron lost a 'veteran' Blenheim IV (R3600) and its crew; the aircraft had previously flown at least forty-eight operations - quite remarkable as only five Blenheims managed to survive fifty or more operations. The pilot, Flight Lieutenant E.N. Steel, was a New

Zealander who had travelled to Britain to join the pre-war R.A.F.

A new squadron, No 226, arrived at Wattisham in late May; it had been recently detached to Coastal Command and operated from Northern Ireland with Fairey Battles. After its crews had converted to Blenheims at Wattisham, the Squadron became operational in June and had the misfortune to lose four crews in just three days in early July whilst engaged on 'Circus' operations, including its Squadron Commander, Wing Commander R.C. Hurst. Another eleven crews went missing on 'Channel Stop' operations and it must be said that the two Wattisham squadrons fared far better in this respect than the other Blenheim squadrons. In August Winston Churchill paid high praise to the Blenheim crews:

> The devotion of these attacks on Rotterdam and other objectives are beyond praise. The Charge of the Light Brigade at Balaclava is eclipsed in brightness by their almost daily deeds of fame.

Blenheim IV – R3600 – of No 110 Squadron being armed and refuelled at R.A.F. Wattisham. After 48 sorties it was shot down on 6th May 1941; all three airmen were killed.

Blenheim IVs attacking Rotterdam docks in July 1941. (via R.P. Scott)

Churchill's reference to 'Rotterdam' related to two daylight attacks on the docks, one in mid-July and the second on 28th August when eight of the eighteen Blenheims were lost (44%!). One of No 226 Squadron's Blenheims crashed on take-off and another was shot down and crashed into the dock.

It was not only the Blenheim crews that operated by day; on rare occasions the Wellington crews were sent on 'Circus' operations and on 9th June two of No 9 Squadron's Wellingtons joined two other Wellingtons and two Stirlings on a reconnaissance operation off the French and Belgian coast. Sadly the two Wellingtons failed to return to Honington; one of them was piloted by the Squadron's Commander, Wing Commander R.C.C. Arnold, MiD, who had been in charge of the Squadron since January. It was later discovered that both aircraft had been shot down by Bf 109s and that the Wing Commander had remained at the controls long enough for his crew to bale out before the aircraft crashed into the sea and before he could escape. The five crewmen were rescued and taken prisoner but only one of the crew of the other Wellington survived. Wing Commander Arnold's selfless sacrifice would be replicated by many bomber captains or 'skippers' in the years ahead.

Such 'conspicuous bravery' was not the sole preserve of the aircrews. On 16/17th May a damaged Wellington of No 9 Squadron returning from Boulogne was forced to make an emergency landing at Honington and crashed perilously close to the bomb dump before bursting into flames.

The Station Commander, Group Captain J.A. Gray, along with the Medical Officer, Squadron Leader J. McCarty, entered the blazing aircraft to extricate two of the crew. For their 'conspicuous bravery' both officers were awarded George Medals. Earlier in the year (29th January) the Station Chaplain at Stradishall, Padre Harrison, had saved a Wellington crew of No 214 Squadron in very similar circumstances; he too was awarded the George Medal.

The first wartime-built airfield in the county opened in June and was sited near the small and then fairly isolated village of Lakenheath. It had been selected as a suitable site early in 1940 and was nearly equidistant between the prime bomber stations of Mildenhall and Feltwell. It was originally a 'decoy' airfield for Feltwell but then it was decided to develop it into a full bomber station with the provision of three concrete runways and two large hangars; on completion it was allocated to Mildenhall as a satellite airfield. However, it did not become fully operational until April 1942 when No 149 Squadron moved in from Mildenhall.

For the British public, who had bravely and valiantly lived through the horrors of the Blitz of the winter of 1940/41, the men of Bomber Command appeared the only military force to be striking back at the enemy, seemingly night after night; the nightly news bulletins were avidly listened to and these brave airmen were held in high regard and esteem. Therefore it was not surprising that when the overtly propagandist film *Target for Tonight* was released in July, it became an instant success and further added lustre to the public's deep admiration of the 'Bomber Men'.

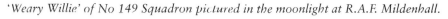

'Weary Willie' of No 149 Squadron pictured in the moonlight at R.A.F. Mildenhall.

Poster for *Target for Tonight*.

This classic documentary was produced by the Crown Film Unit and had been directed by Harry Watts. Much of the filming had been undertaken at Mildenhall (renamed Millerton for the film); one crewman recalls that the airfield looked 'like a film set'. Unlike *The Lion Has Wings*, there were no professional actors taking part in the film, only R.A.F. personnel. The public warmed to the crew of *F for Freddie* (actually Wellington IA P2517 of No 149 Squadron) but without doubt the 'star' of the film was 'Squadron Leader Dixon', who was actually Squadron Leader Charles 'Percy' or 'Pick' Pickard, D.S.O., D.F.C. He was already a very experienced pilot and leader having completed a tour of operations with No 99 Squadron and was now in joint command of No 311 (Czech) Squadron, which had been formed at Honington in July 1940 but was currently based at East Wretham. Pickard was destined to become one of the most famous and legendary 'heroes' of Bomber Command. He added to his fame with the audacious raid on the Bruneval radar station in northern France in February 1942. Almost exactly two years later he lost his life as an acting Group Captain leading Mosquitos of No 140 Wing in a daring attack on the Gestapo prison at Amiens in northern France to free Resistance prisoners awaiting execution. Percy Pickard was twenty-eight years old at the time of his death; he had completed over one hundred operations and had also been awarded two Bars to his D.S.O. and the Czech Military Cross. Basil Embry, who was his Commander-in-Chief at the time, gave him a fulsome eulogy:

> It is impossible to measure Charles Pickard's loss to the R.A.F. and Britain, but in courage, devotion to duty, fighting spirit and powers of really leading, he stood out for me as one of the great airmen of the war and as a shining example of British manhood. I always felt he was part of a character from an earlier Elizabethan age.

At the time of the release of *Target for Tonight*, neither the public nor indeed the crews were aware of a damning report on the inadequacies of the strategic bombing offensive, which was presented to the War Cabinet on 18th August. The now famous (or infamous) Butt Report had been compiled by D.M. Butt of the War Cabinet Secretariat and had been expressly ordered by Lord Cherwell, the Prime Minister's scientific adviser. After examining over four thousand aerial photographs taken on night operations during June and July, the Report concluded that only one in four crews that had claimed to have bombed the target had actually been within five miles of it. Over the Ruhr the figure fell alarmingly to one crew in ten. Furthermore, as the precious cameras were reserved for only the experienced crews, the situation was even more serious. It was also known from debriefings that on average one third of the crews had not actually reached the target area for a variety of reasons. With mounting losses, from 3.9% in May to 7% in August, and faced with such damning evidence, the future of the Command's strategic bombing offensive looked rather bleak, especially as losses of aircraft and airmen began to further increase in the autumn.

Group Captain C.P. 'Pick' Pickard, D.S.O., 2 Bars, D.F.C., Czech Military Cross, with his faithful dog 'Ming'.

A rather unique squadron was formed at Newmarket Heath on 25th August – No 138 (Special Duties) – from the nucleus of No 1419 (formerly 119) Flight, which had been operating from Stradishall since the previous October. Its first Commander was Wing Commander E.V. Knowles, D.F.C., who would be replaced by Wing Commander W.K. Farley in November. To all intents and purposes it was the operational arm of the Special Operations Executive (S.O.E.), which had been formed as a so-called 'Fourth Arm' to undertake industrial and military sabotage in the enemy-occupied countries. The Squadron, like No 1419 Flight before it, was required to parachute arms and supplies to the Resistance forces as well as dropping and picking up agents and for these tasks it was equipped with Armstrong Whitworth Whitley Vs, some Westland Lysanders and a couple of Handley Page Halifaxes. On 17/18th February one of the Flight's Whitley Vs had been lost, the first aircraft missing on 'special duties'. The Squadron's first operation took place on 29/30th August when a Whitley V operated over Châteauroux with none other than Squadron Leader Pickard acting as co-pilot; he was then stationed at No 3 Group Headquarters and was supposed to be resting from operations! After completing no less than fifty operations from Newmarket, the Squadron moved to Stradishall on 16th December, where it remained until March 1942.

By September 1941 Bomber Command had completed two years of war and during this time it had dropped thirty-five thousand tons of bombs for the loss of one thousand and three hundred aircraft, which equated to twenty-seven tons of bombs dropped for each crew lost in action. One year later the Command dropped half that total quantity in just *two months* for the loss of five hundred and three aircraft, or thirty-four tons for each missing crew. This comparison gives some idea of the rapid advance and development of Bomber Command in just twelve months.

During the month, despite steadily mounting losses, over one hundred and fifty bombers were despatched on twelve nights to various targets in Germany and Italy. Over three thousand sorties were made for the loss of one hundred and fifty aircraft (4.9%), which was only just below what Command chiefs considered a 'tolerable loss or sustainable rate' of 5%, although even at this rate the planned expansion of the Command would be seriously jeopardised. Many of these losses were the result of a greatly strengthened German night fighter force and the establishment of what became known as the *Kammhuber Belt* (from the German Commander, Josef Kammhuber). It was a line of searchlights stretching from Denmark to Holland and was allied to a chain of 'boxes' – areas of the skies where the night fighters could be controlled from the ground by radar. This proved to be a formidable obstacle for the Command's crews; in fact, the German High Command claimed that in one year the destruction of enemy bombers had increased tenfold from forty-two to four hundred and twenty-one in 1941.

The reputation and prestige of the Command's airmen in the eyes of the British public was further enhanced in October with the publication by the Air Ministry of *Bomber Command*. It was a booklet of most persuasive text and excellent vibrant photographs, which described the Command's bombing offensive up to July 1941. The booklet was published in two editions with exactly the same text but with different covers: one featured a black and white photograph of a Short Stirling and the other a full col-

The Air Ministry booklet 'Bomber Command' published in October 1941

our reproduction of a striking painting of a Whitley over a target at night. In retrospect the tone of the booklet might be considered overly jingoistic and that it greatly exaggerated the effectiveness of this offensive, certainly in the light of the Butt Report. Nevertheless it was unstinting in its praise of the aircrews, devoting two chapters to them and their preparations for an operation. Quite how they felt about being described as 'gentlemen of the shade, minions of the moon' has not to my knowledge been recorded! However, the booklet concluded with:

> One thing is certain, Bomber Command will allow no pause, no breathing space. Our attack will go on, fierce because it is relentless, deadly because it is so sure.

Brave and stirring words indeed, considering that barely one month later the whole future of Bomber Command and its bombing offensive was under close scrutiny, consideration and debate.

The use of a photograph of a Short Stirling on the cover of one of the editions of *Bomber Command* illustrated the Command's pride in its first four-engine heavy bomber, which had entered operations with No 7 Squadron at Oakington back in January. The first Stirling Is arrived at Mildenhall on 12th October, when No 149 Squadron became the third squadron to be equipped with the new bomber.

The prototype had first flown in May 1939 but it was twelve months before the first production Stirling (N363) emerged. There had never been another aeroplane quite like the Stirling. Compared with its competitors, the Lancaster and the Halifax, it was the tallest (nearly 23 ft from ground to cockpit), the longest at 87 ft and with the shortest wingspan at 99 ft. Without doubt the aircraft looked ungainly on the ground and at first sight could be rather daunting to new crews, rather a giant compared to a Wellington. However, in flight it proved to be highly manoeuvrable, gaining the sobriquet 'fighter bomber', and not solely on account of the eight 0.303 machine-guns in three turrets; by repute it could turn inside a Spitfire. It had also proved to be a most sturdy aircraft, able to sustain considerable damage. The Stirling had a range of some 740 miles, with a maximum bomb load of 14,000 lbs. However, with a cruising speed of 200 mph and a relatively low operational altitude of 12,000 ft, it suffered proportionally higher losses than both the Lancaster and Halifax. Later it was vulnerable from above when operating with Lancasters, which released their bombs from a far higher altitude. Although Air Chief Marshal Harris had a poor opinion of the Stirling, they in fact served Bomber Command well and ultimately all of No 3 Group's squadrons would be equipped with Stirlings. When their time as an operational bomber came to an end they operated successfully as transports, glider tugs and troop carriers and over two thousand, seven hundred and thirty were produced in various marks.

During most of October and November the crews of No 149 Squadron were engaged in conversion training and it was not until 26/27th November that the first Stirling crews went into action when two accompanied six of the Squadron's Wellingtons to Ostend. All eight aircraft arrived back safely. The far heavier Stirlings were not suited to the grass runways at Mildenhall and they quickly turned the airfield into a quagmire. The pre-war decision not to provide concrete runways for the bomber stations was coming home to roost, thus it was that the Stirlings began to use Lakenheath more and more for operations.

On 2nd November the last anti-shipping operations by the Blenheim crews were mounted; since March almost one hundred and forty Blenheims had been lost in action and such high casualty losses could no longer be condoned. In any case, the days of the Blenheims in Bomber Command were now numbered. In late October, three Douglas Boston IIIs had arrived at Wattisham for tests and trials with No 226 Squadron, while its crews had been taken off operations; the Squadron had completed two hundred and forty-one Blenheim sorties for the loss of sixteen aircraft (6.6%). In early December the Squadron moved to Swanton Morley in Norfolk.

Besides the most disturbing findings of the Butt Report, what really should have sounded the alarm bells at the Command Headquarters and along the corridors of the Air Ministry, was the operation mounted on 7/8th November when almost four hundred bombers were despatched to targets in Berlin, Cologne and Mannheim; the largest number ever sent out on a single night. Of the one hundred and sixty-nine crews sent to Berlin less than half reached the city. The damage inflicted was quite minimal but sadly twenty-one crews failed to return (12.4%), the heaviest loss of the war. Another seven aircraft were missing from the Münster raid; almost two hundred airmen missing in action on a single night. Considering such losses, the three Suffolk Wellington squadrons fared better than most. No 149 lost one crew and a badly damaged Wellington of No 214 Squadron ditched in the sea off Holland; all of the crew finally came ashore in their dinghy at the Isle of Wight three days later and the pilot, Pilot Officer L.B. Ercolani, was awarded the D.S.O. in January 1942.

No force could sustain such losses for any length of time and still survive. In the previous four months, four hundred and twenty six aircraft had been lost in action, very close to the *total* strength of Bomber Command at the beginning of 1941. It was perhaps not surprising that morale in the squadrons was at a low ebb. The War Cabinet, faced with such losses and the findings of the Butt Report, decided that the bomber offensive, at least in its present form, should be virtually halted to allow time to consider a new policy. Air Marshal Peirse was informed that only limited operations to less well-defended targets were to be carried out over the coming winter months; certainly no major operation was sent to Berlin for almost fifteen months. Nevertheless, despite the so-called 'limited operations' seven Wellingtons and twenty-seven airmen were lost from Suffolk airfields up until the end of the year.

The second new bomber squadron to be formed in the county was No 419 at Mildenhall on 15th December. Needless to say, it was equipped with Wellingtons and was mainly composed of airmen of the Royal Canadian Air Force and as such was the third R.C.A.F. bomber squadron to serve in Bomber Command. Wing Commander John 'Moose' Fulton, D.F.C., was appointed its first Commander. Fulton hailed from British Columbia but had joined the R.A.F. in 1935 and by October 1940 he had completed his first operational tour with No 10 Squadron. He was regarded as one of the most able leaders in Bomber Command, who led his crews by his fine example and, as a Canadian, was considered an ideal choice to command the new Squadron.

When No 110 Squadron returned to Wattisham from Lossiemouth shortly after Christmas (28th), it was a rather sad homecoming. On the previous day four out of six crews had been lost whilst engaged in the support of the Allied Commando landings at Vaags in Norway. These losses were a harsh and bitter end to the year for the Wattisham Squadron.

Without doubt 1941 had been a testing and costly time for Bomber Command, with almost fifteen hundred aircraft lost in action and training accidents; but more to the point was the loss of so many experienced airmen: over four hundred and sixty failed to return to their Suffolk airfields with just seventy-six (16%) surviving as prisoners of war. Such losses in many ways appear more distressing because of the relatively small number of crews involved, at least compared with the awesome strength of the Command in the following years. It should not be forgotten that these crews did not have the benefit of improved aircraft, sophisticated navigational aids or the target-marking procedures, which were just on the horizon. Nevertheless, the many and varied operations conducted during the year ultimately led the way to those more successful and acclaimed operations of 1942 and 1943. One might even say that these airmen were really the first 'Pathfinders', at least in the widest sense of the word.

Chapter 5

'The Right Man in the Right Place at the Right Time'

(JANUARY TO JUNE 1942)

The year 1942 was a most auspicious and crucial one for Bomber Command. It rose, almost like a phoenix, from its nadir at the close of 1941 to become what Winston Churchill later described as 'our immensely powerful weapon'. The year witnessed the arrival of Air Marshal Arthur T. Harris as its Commander-in-Chief; his name is forever associated with Bomber Command and under his direction and dynamic leadership the legendary 'thousand bomber' raids were launched followed by a heavy and sustained bombing offensive of Germany. Two new navigational aids – *Gee* and *Oboe* were introduced along with improved target marking techniques to be perfected by the *elite d'corps*, the Pathfinder Force (P.F.F.), which was formed in August. Two of the outstanding bombers of the Second World War – the Lancaster and the Mosquito – also entered service with the Command.

On 8th January Air Marshal Sir Richard Peirse was relieved of his post for what was described as a 'special appointment' – Commander of the Allied Air Force in India. Peirse had been effectively made the scapegoat for the ills of the Command, though it could be said that few were of his making. Jack Baldwin, erstwhile Commander of No 3 Group, was given the temporary command. The Air Staff knew the very officer they wanted for the top post, Arthur Harris, who had been the Commander of No 5 Group from September 1939 to November 1940. However, he was then in Washington, U.S.A. leading an Air Ministry delegation and would not be available until mid-February.

During January the strict limitation on operations was still in force and although a number of German targets were attacked, they were rather low-key operations with just over six hundred and seventy aircraft being despatched to Germany during the whole month. There was one Suffolk squadron, No 138 (Special Duties) at Stradishall, not subject to the restrictions and its crews continued their clandestine operations, which were conducted in the utmost secrecy. On 28/29th January one of its Whitley Vs failed to return; it was believed lost at sea and there were no survivors from the seven-man crew. That same night Squadron Leader J. 'Whippy' Nesbitt-Dufont left in a black Lysander III for a field at Issoudun about one hundred miles south-west of Paris. The operation was codenamed *Beryl II*. He had one S.O.E. agent

A black Westland Lysander III. No 138 (Special Duties) Squadron at R.A.F. Stradishall was equipped with some of these aircraft; one was lost in action on 28/29th January 1942.

on board and was due to pick up two 'passengers' at Issoudun. However, due to severe icing, he was forced to make a crash-landing shortly after he had taken off from Issoudun. He successfully destroyed the Lysander and managed to evade capture for a month before he and his two 'passengers' were picked up by an Anson of No 161 (Special Duties) Squadron on 1st March. This Squadron had only just formed at Newmarket Heath about two weeks earlier. On his return, Nesbitt-Dufont was awarded the D.S.O. He survived the war as a Wing Commander and related his experiences whilst in France in his book *Black Lysander*, which was published in 1973 just two years before his death.

These two Special Duties squadrons moved to Graveley in March before finding a permanent home at Tempsford, Bedfordshire. It should not be forgotten that the brave and intrepid airmen of both squadrons were engaged in their own very special and lonely 'secret' war and were members of Bomber Command just as much as their more heralded colleagues of the 'proper' bomber squadrons. In October 1942 Wing Commander Pickard became the Commander of No 161 Squadron, which added another chapter to his illustrious R.A.F. career.

The port of Brest and the three German vessels – *Scharnhorst*, *Gneisenau* and *Prinz Eugen* – occupied many crews during January and early February; the crews nicknamed the two battlecruisers 'Salmon' and 'Gluckstein' from a well-known chain of tobacconists although officially they were codenamed *Toads*! No less than eleven raids were made during the period with the final one taking place on 6/7th February when three Wellingtons were lost, which brought the total casualties in these operations, which had been ongoing for almost a year, to one hundred and twenty-seven. Over three thousand, four hundred tons of bombs had been dropped without any substantial damage to the three vessels. Five days later (22nd) the German vessels made their bold escape from Brest. They were first sighted in the English Channel in the late morning and immediately Operation *Fuller* was activated. This was a joint Admiralty and Air Ministry plan, which had been in place since the previous April for just this eventuality. The German Admiral had selected an ideal day; appalling weather conditions in the Channel and heavy low cloud afforded the flotilla the maximum concealment.

During the afternoon no fewer than two hundred and fifty-two bombers were engaged in what proved to be a futile attempt to prevent the vessels' escape. This was the largest daylight operation mounted by the Command so far, but few crews located the flotilla let alone bombed the vessels. Also

The crew of Stirling W7455 'OJ-B' of No 149 Squadron in January 1942. The aircraft survived until September 1943. (Imperial War Museum)

engaged in the operation were forty fighter squadrons and units of the Fleet Air Arm; one F.A.A. pilot, Lieutenant Commander E. Esmonde, D.S.O., was awarded a posthumous Victoria Cross for his actions. The infamous 'Channel Dash', as the British press called it, was a most inglorious episode for the Royal Navy and the R.A.F. The only damage the three vessels sustained was from mines but, nevertheless, all made it safely to a German port.

Fifteen bombers were lost on this abortive operation; three of the crews came from Suffolk airfields. No 110 Squadron lost its thirty-eighth and last Blenheim in action. The ages of the three crewmen were a stark reminder of the number of very young men serving in the Command; the pilot was just eighteen years old and the other two barely twenty years old! The Squadron was shortly stood down from operations and in March it was posted to India, hence 'Hyderabad' in its title. The Squadron had completed two and a half years of continuous service with Bomber Command since the second day of the war. The Canadian squadron, No 419, lost its first two aircraft in action, and all but one of the twelve airmen killed in action were Canadians.

No 214 Squadron at Stradishall also lost a Wellington and, sadly, it was captained by the Squadron Commander, Wing Commander R.D.B. MacFadden, D.F.C., who had been in charge since the previous September. Only one of the crew, Sergeant R. Murray, survived as a prisoner of war. He later related the horrifying ordeal. They ditched in the North Sea and only five of the crew managed to get into the dinghy before it was swept away by the sinking aircraft. During the next seventy-two hours that the dinghy drifted, Murray watched whilst his four fellow crewmen slowly succumbed to the intense cold, lost consciousness and then died – a most harrowing experience.

However, Bomber Command was not quite finished with the three German

The crew of 'H-Harry' of No 419 Squadron, R.C.A.F. at R.A.F. Mildenhall on 9th February 1942. From left: Squadron Leader F.W.S. Turner, Pilot Officer K.E. Hobson, Flight Sergeants G.P. Fowler, C.A. Robson, N.G. Arthur and H.J. Dell – all R.C.A.F. airmen. By the end of July 1942 three of these airmen – Pilot Officer Hobson and Flight Sergeants Arthur and Dell – had been killed in action. (via S.L. McDonald)

battleships; on 22nd/23rd February Wilhelmshaven, where it was thought that the vessels were undergoing repairs, was attacked, but the target area was covered with heavy cloud making accurate bombing almost impossible. Quickly the Command's attention was directed to Kiel, which according to photographic evidence housed the *Scharnhorst* and *Gneisenau*. The port was attacked on the three successive nights from the 25/26th, in what were reputed to be 'revenge raids' for the German vessels' audacious escape. The first Kiel raid had some success, when the *Gneisenau*, which was in the floating dock undergoing repairs, received a direct hit causing sufficient damage to ensure that the vessel never sailed again as a fighting vessel – a small recompense for all the crews' efforts. Nevertheless, in the three Kiel raids another six crews were lost; the Command's attempts to cripple these German battleships had been rather costly in men and machines.

On 14th February Bomber Command received an important and pivotal Directive: '... it has been decided that the primary objective of your operations should be focused on the morale of the enemy civil population and in particular the industrial workers ...'. Four major targets were identified – Essen, Duisburg, Düsseldorf and Cologne – along with eighteen alternatives; furthermore the Directive added a caveat 'to use the utmost resources at all times'. The Air Staff, particularly Sir Charles Portal, sought clarification of the precise meaning of the Directive – 'the built-up areas' and *not* specifically 'the docks, railways and factories'? Yes, this was officially confirmed, thus 'area bombing' had been officially sanctioned even before Air Marshal Harris was appointed.

It was eight days later (22nd) that the very man to implement such an outright bombing offensive arrived at the Command's Headquarters at High Wycombe: 'Bomber' Harris had entered the fray. He proved to be inexorable in his prosecution of the bombing offensive and pursued it with a grim and ruthless determination right up until the end of the war. Certainly it could be said that he was 'the right man, in the right place, at the right time'. 'Butch' Harris, as he was known to his crews, gained a fierce, unswerving and undying loyalty from those airmen (and airwomen) under his control, which remained steadfast throughout the war and still survives today with the dwindling band of the Command's veterans. Without doubt his arrival ushered in a new era for Bomber Command. He famously quoted from the Book of *Hosea*, chapter 8 verse 7: 'They have sown the wind; and they shall reap the whirlwind', which perhaps neatly summed up his attitude to the job ahead.

Heavy "Stirling" bombers raid the Nazi Baltic port of Lübeck and leave the docks ablaze

BACK THEM UP

A National Savings campaign poster depicting Stirlings over Lübeck on 28/29th March 1942

*Bomb aimer in a Wellington: a still from
Target for Tonight.*

During his first month of command Harris carefully took stock of his resources. The *effective* strength stood at three hundred and seventy-eight heavy and medium bombers and crews, of which over 80% were the trusty 'Wimpys'. Furthermore he had fifty-six Blenheims and twenty-two Bostons, but these light bombers were virtually dismissed from his mind and they would not really figure in his plans; in his view their only role was night intruder raids against enemy fighter airfields to assist his precious bombers and to engage the *Luftwaffe*'s night fighters. In late February Harris summed up the position as 'a lack of suitable aircraft in sufficient numbers and the deficiency of trained crews'. With typical verve and dynamism he proceeded to improve the situation.

The makeup of the heavy and medium bomber crews was radically changed; the second pilot was dispensed with and a new designation of navigator was introduced with the navigation of the aircraft being his sole responsibility. In future the pilot would be assisted by a flight engineer. Bomb aiming was now to be performed by an 'air bomber', more popularly known as a 'bomb aimer', and the roles of air gunner and wireless operator were separated. These changes gave each member of the crew more specialised and thorough training in his specific duties and it has been suggested that without them, 'Bomber Command would certainly have never approached the degree of efficiency which it ultimately achieved'.

Harris was fortunate that the first new navigational aid, *Gee* (Ground Electrical Engineering), was ready for operational use; it was a device that enabled the navigator to guide an aircraft to a target. The *Gee* box received two sets of pulse signals from three separate ground stations and computed the time difference between the receipts of these signals to give an almost instant fix. *Gee* was relatively simple to use but it did have a range limitation of about three hundred and fifty miles, which covered the Ruhr Valley and some of the north-west German ports. *Gee* was an immediate success with the crews, perhaps because it was a valuable aid in locating their home airfield in poor weather conditions. It was thought that *Gee* would have an operational life of about six months before the enemy devised the means to jam its signals, which in fact they had done by August.

In order to obtain the maximum advantage of the new device from the hundred and fifty aircraft then equipped with a *Gee* box, a new bombing procedure was introduced known as *Shaker*. The bomber force was divided into three groups – Illuminators, Target Markers and Followers. The Illuminators, all with *Gee,* would be the first over the target dropping flares at ten-second intervals backed up by high explosives. The Target Markers would be the next on the scene; they dropped a maximum load of incendiaries to provide a concentrated area of fire for the Followers some fifteen minutes later with their high explosives. This *Shaker* technique was the precursor of the formation of the P.F.F. later in the summer.

Everything was now in place for the battle to commence. Although Harris's early months at Bomber Command are forever remembered for the remarkable Lübeck raid and the three famous 'thousand bomber' raids, it was Essen that was selected for his first heavy bombing offensive. In no less than eight raids from 8/9th March to 12/13th April, followed by five nights in June, this city was attacked by over three thousand, one hundred and sixty aircraft – an early example of the dogged and almost obsessive determination of the new Commander-in-Chief.

Essen had a population of six hundred and sixty thousand and was sited in the Ruhr Valley. It was considered the very heart of Germany's heavy and munitions industries and was dominated

Total devastation – the Krupps factories in Essen, 1945. (via M.J. Hughes)

by the massive Krupps armaments complex in the centre of the city which covered several hundred acres. The Air Staff considered Essen as 'the supreme target' and it was more heavily defended by flak and searchlight batteries than any other German target but for Berlin; the crews called it 'Flak City'. Before the crews even reached the Ruhr they had to run the gauntlet of large numbers of night fighters based mainly in Holland and Belgium and once over the Ruhr they encountered an almost permanent industrial haze, even on moonlit nights, which greatly hampered target marking and accurate bombing. By March 1945 Essen had been bombed on thirty-seven nights, making it the most heavily bombed German city, even more so than Berlin.

The first major raid on Essen was launched on 8/9th March and it was the first time that *Gee* was used on a major operation; unfortunately the bombing was not very satisfactory, nor indeed were the subsequent raids with only fairly minimal damage being sustained by the Krupps factories. In these thirteen operations one hundred and forty-eight aircraft (4.7%) were lost and many of the airmen killed are buried in the Rechswald Forest War Cemetery near Kleve. Here are buried the largest number of airmen (three thousand, nine hundred and seventy-one) of any war cemetery in Germany.

The five bomber squadrons - Nos 9, 109, 149, 214 and 419 - then operating from Suffolk airfields were all engaged in these Essen raids and a total of sixteen aircraft were lost and ninety-four airmen posted as missing in action, of whom only five survived as prisoners of war. It seems a trifle invidious to pick out just a few airmen who lost their lives in this offensive, but it does illustrate the quality, experience and determination of the bomber crews at this stage of the war. No 9 Squadron at Honington lost two crews on the first Essen raid and only one airman survived – Flying Officer R.F. Hoult; he was picked up by a fishing trawler after surviving for thirty-three hours in the North Sea. Two nights later No 149 Squadron at Lakenheath lost a most experienced pilot, Squadron Leader L.W. Colman, D.F.C. and Bar, a New Zealander who had joined the pre-war R.A.F.; he was the first airman from that country to be awarded a Bar to his D.F.C. Then on 12/13th April Sergeant F. Davidson of No 9 Squadron was killed; just four days later it was announced that he had been awarded the D.F.M. for 'his courage and skill on recent operations'.

It was a sad fact of operational life that virtually every bomber squadron suffered a heavy and crippling loss on a single night's operation, really a matter of its crews being in the wrong place at the wrong time. Tragically this happened to No 214 Squadron on 1st/2nd April. On this night the Command Headquarters launched an experimental raid, a low-level attack on railway targets at Hanau and Lohr to the west of Frankfurt. It proved to be a disastrous and costly failure, or in the words of the crews – 'a real shaky do' ('a bungled affair'). Out of the forty-nine crews taking part only twenty-two claimed to have bombed and twelve of the thirty-five Wellingtons were lost (34%), with No 214 Squadron losing seven out of fourteen aircraft – forty-five airmen missing in action; by far the Squadron's heaviest single loss of the war.

The first real and tangible bombing success for the new Commander-in-Chief came on 28/29th March when the old Hanseatic port on the Baltic coast, Lübeck, was bombed by one hundred and ninety-one crews of the two hundred and forty-three taking part. In a matter of two hours over four hundred tons of bombs were dropped, two-thirds of them incendiaries, and the narrow streets and timbered buildings in the *Aldstradt* (old town) were engulfed in flames. It was perhaps a perfect example of 'area bombing' and the Air Ministry claimed that one hundred and ninety acres had been destroyed, the first time acreage had been used to quantify bomb damage. The successful raid was greeted with great acclaim by the British press and the public, who were desperate for some evidence that the country was striking back at Germany. Thirteen aircraft (5.1%) were lost, including an all-R.C.A.F. crew of No 419 Squadron, whose Wellington III fell to a ferocious head-on attack by Bf 110s, one of which was believed to have been shot down; one of the Wellington's crew was killed and the other five were captured. The severity and horror of the bombing shocked the German High Command and Hitler personally endorsed retaliatory raids on similar ancient English cities or 'any listed in *Baedeker*', hence the heavy raids on Exeter, Norwich, Bath and Canterbury.

One month later another Baltic port, Rostock, was bombed on four consecutive nights from 23rd to 26th April, with over five hundred and twenty crews in action over the four nights and very light losses – eight aircraft (1.5%). The damage inflicted on the port and town was even more devastating: one hundred and thirty acres laid waste, or 60% of the town. For the first time the German High Command called these raids *Terrorangriff* ('terror raids'). They were a portent for the German people of all the horrors of heavy bombing that they would suffer in the months ahead.

Most of the Wellington squadrons had been or were in the process of exchanging their Mark ICs for Mark IIIs, which were powered by Bristol

Hercules engines that produced an increase in speed. The aircraft's armament had also been improved with the addition of two extra 0.303 inch guns. The Mark III extended the operational life of the Wellington as a front-line bomber.

During this period more and more of the Wellington and Stirling crews were employed on mine-laying or 'Gardening' as it was code-named, which had now become an increasingly important aspect of the Command's operational schedule. Air Marshal Harris had somewhat reluctantly agreed with the Admiralty to lay at least one thousand mines a month. 'Gardening' involved the crews 'planting vegetables' (mines) from a height of about 600 ft in a specific location, each of which was given a horticultural name such as *Spinach* (Baltic Sea), *Artichokes* (Lorient), *Forget-me-knots* (Kiel Canal) and so on. The publication *Bomber Command* described these operations thus:

> It calls for great skill and resolution. Moreover the crew do not have the satisfaction of seeing the partial results of their work. There is no coloured explosion; no burgeoning of fire…At best all they see is a splash on the surface of a dark and inhospitable sea.

Stirling crews at R.A.F. Lakenheath being briefed for a 'Gardening' operation.

A Wellington III of No 419 Squadron receiving its 4,000 lb 'Cookie' bomb before the Cologne raid. (R.A.F. Museum)

Despite this, most crews welcomed the operations; they considered them light relief from targets in Germany because they felt that their chances of survival were far higher. But on 17/18th May, when sixty crews from No 3 Group were engaged on mine-laying, there was a particularly strong presence of enemy night fighters and seven aircraft were lost (11.6%); three were Stirlings of No 149 Squadron, now permanently operating from Lakenheath and another was a Wellington III of No 419 Squadron at Mildenhall. Mine-laying comprised 15% of the Command's total operational sorties of the war and they continued right up to 25/26th April 1945. A post-war analysis claimed that over four hundred and ninety enemy vessels had been sunk by mines dropped by Bomber Command but at a cost of four hundred and ninety-one aircraft with the majority of their crews being posted 'missing at sea'.

In April (6th) Lakenheath was returned to operational status when No 149 Squadron moved in from Mildenhall, although for a couple of months the Squadron's Stirlings had used the airfield on a detached basis. Towards the end of the month (20th) the county's last surviving Blenheim squadron, No 18, returned to Wattisham after night flying training in Scotland. Henceforth its crews would operate by night on 'intruder' raids over Holland and

Belgium mainly to attack enemy fighter airfields and occasionally other targets like power stations. In fact the Squadron lost its first crew on 28/29th April when six Blenheims were sent to bomb Langenburgge power station; all three airmen were killed.

The city of Cologne from the air in 1945. Amidst such devastation the Cathedral stands out proudly.

In May Air Marshal Harris conceived a plan that was bold, audacious and breathtaking in concept, especially considering the strength of his Command at that time, which was little more than four hundred aircraft and crews. He proposed to gather a force of one thousand bombers and send them to a German city on a single night; previously the highest number had been two hundred and seventy-two back in early April. His plan, code-named 'Millennium', gained the approval of the Air Ministry and ultimately Winston Churchill, despite the fact that the losses on such an operation were projected to be one hundred aircraft.

In order to arrive at the magical figure of 'one thousand' Harris sought the help of Coastal Command. He also made a brave decision to include a large number of trainee crews of the Operational Training Units and Conversion Flights; these ultimately supplied a third of the bomber force. For this operation the Command introduced a new concept – the bomber stream – whereby all the aircraft would fly a common route at the same speed both to and from the target. Furthermore, each crew was allotted a specific height band and time slot to lessen the risk of collision. The actual time for the bombing was reduced to ninety minutes; a quite revolutionary decision which many felt could not be achieved. By 26th May all the plans had been formalised, the port of Hamburg had been selected as the target and everything now waited on a favourable weather forecast for the end of the month. It was not until the 30th that Harris decided to change to his second choice, Cologne, and shortly after noon on that fateful day, the message 'Operation Plan Cologne' was relayed to the fifty-three bomber airfields engaged in this massive operation, of which five were in Suffolk – Mildenhall, Stradishall, Lakenheath, Honington and Wattisham.

The briefing of the crews took place at 6 pm and when they were told that Cologne was to be the target, there was considerable relief as many felt that it was going to be Berlin. But the cheers that greeted the news that they were to be a part of a 'thousand bomber' force were euphoric, although a little tempered by the real threat of collisions whilst flying in such a massive force. The news that the Command's 'boffins' had computed the collision factor as just one per hour over the target area, or two in total, raised many a smile and far more sceptical comments!

On this momentous night one thousand and forty-seven aircraft left for Cologne with No 3 Group supplying the largest number of any Group – two hundred and twenty-two or over one quarter – of which eighty-one flew from Suffolk airfields. Few of the Group's crews were aware that their Commander, Jack Baldwin, would accompany them in a Stirling of No 218 Squadron based at Marham. Certainly, if Air Marshal Harris had known of this he would have forbidden it. As the four Suffolk bomber stations were the closest to the target, Nos 9, 149, 214 and 419 Squadrons were in the vanguard of the bomber stream. They were also some of the earliest squadrons to be equipped with Gee and thus would be part of the incendiary

No 18 Squadron was the last Blenheim squadron to operate from R.A.F. Wattisham and its crews flew the last Blenheim raid for Bomber Command on 17/18th August 1942.

force dropping their 4 lb incendiary canisters along with high explosives. To support this major operation, forty-nine Blenheims of No 2 Group were sent out earlier to attack night fighter airfields in the path of the bomber stream. Twenty-four Blenheims of Nos 18 and 13 Squadrons left from Wattisham; the latter was an Army Co-Operation squadron which had been specifically detached to Wattisham for the operation.

In just ninety minutes almost nine hundred crews dropped one thousand, four hundred and fifty tons of bombs; two-thirds of them were incendiaries and the resultant fires could be seen from a distance of some one hundred and fifty miles and burned for several days. A total of forty-one aircraft were lost (3.9%) and in the light of this it could be said that the Suffolk squadrons escaped fairly lightly, especially as the highest losses (4.1%) were suffered by the incendiary force. Both Nos 149 and 419 Squadrons returned unscathed; No 9 Squadron lost two Wellington IIIs, one to flak and the other to night fighters over Eindhoven, Holland. The first Wellington, piloted by Sergeant S.A. Langton, who was on his thirtieth operation, had to force-land in Belgium on its return. Langton and Flight Sergeant E.T. Walsh were badly injured as they were thrown from the aircraft when it collided with trees. Both airmen, along with two others, survived as prisoners of war; unfortunately the tail gunner, Sergeant K.R. Paxman, was killed. He had been with the Squadron for only a matter of days, it was the first time that he had served in a bomber and it was within days of his twenty-second birthday. A Stirling crew of No 214 Squadron was lost over Germany when the aircraft's tail was sheered off in a collision with a Wellington; both aircraft crashed. The 'boffins' had been proved right: just two aircraft were lost in collisions over the target area. Another one of the Squadron's Stirlings, returning to Stradishall some four hours after it had left, crash-landed on the airfield; all of the crew escaped unharmed.

The Cologne operation was considered an outstanding success, it was hailed as the 'World's Biggest Air Raid' and claimed to be the first Allied victory of the war. The country heaped praise on its 'heroic airmen' and Bomber Command's standing in the eyes of the public could not have been any higher. Air Marshal Harris became an instant celebrity and he was knighted four days later. The Cologne raid was an important milestone for Bomber Command and it confirmed its arrival as a major bombing force. As the thousands upon thousands of leaflets dropped over Germany in the weeks ahead declared, '*Die Offensive der Royal Air Force in ihren neuen Form hat beiggen* [The Offensive of the Royal Air Force in its new form has begun]'.

Crews on their way to their aircraft. Despite the heavy losses suffered in June, the official caption reads: 'Their hearts are high'.

Harris was keen to maintain the momentum established by the Cologne success; on 1st/2nd June, Essen was the target for the second 'thousand' raid, although the total number of aircraft fell short by forty-four. Like all the previous Essen raids it was considered a failure and Harris was forced to wait almost a month before he and his Command were in a position to mount a third 'thousand' raid. In the meantime his crews were in action over Bremen, Emden and, of course, Essen, but now the losses began to increase quite alarmingly. Nevertheless, on 25/26th June Bremen was the target for one thousand and sixty-seven aircraft, exceeding that of the Cologne operation. This figure had been made possible by the addition of over one hundred crews of Coastal Command, which were only included on the direct order of Winston Churchill. Quite remarkably the time over the target had been reduced to sixty-five minutes and although the bombing was an improvement on the Essen raid it was not particularly impressive. In total, fifty-five aircraft (4.9%) were lost and quite obviously Harris was not pleased with the results as Bremen was targeted again on 27/28th and 29/30th, with the loss of another twenty-five crews.

The thirteen major raids during June had resulted in the Command suffering its heaviest losses of the war with over two hundred aircraft being lost in action; one aviation historian described the crews as being 'the poor bloody infantry of the air' – echoes of the First World War. Certainly, with a casualty rate hovering around 5%, it meant that the crews had about a 40% chance of surviving a tour of thirty operations and less than a 20% chance of completing the required two tours of a total of fifty operations. It would be fair to say that morale on bomber squadrons was beginning to suffer as the crews saw more and more of their friends and colleagues go missing.

During June the Suffolk squadrons lost in total nineteen crews, several including a number of very experienced airmen. Flight Sergeant J.M. Dalton, R.C.A.F., of No 419 Squadron was lost along with his crew on 5/6th over Essen; he was on his thirtieth operation. When Emden was bombed on successive nights – 19th to 21st – Squadron Leader F. Nixey, D.S.O., of No 214 Squadron at the age of twenty-two one of the youngest Squadron Leaders in the Command was killed. Also lost in these Emden operations was Wing Commander L.V. James, D.F.C., the new Commander of No 9 Squadron; he had already completed twenty-seven operations although this one was the first with his new squadron.

Despite the steadily mounting losses Harris was very positive and up-beat, declaring, 'We are the only people who can win the war. And we *are* winning it'. The *Bomber Command Review*, an official publication which was produced quarterly to keep the Commanders in the field aware of what was happening, was quite clear about the way ahead. The Command's priorities were clearly stated:

> **... to destroy the enemy's ports and ships, the mainspring of his offensive against our ocean convoys and also to inflict maximum damage on German and German-controlled industries...it is now our policy to create havoc to those German towns, which house the works or whose efforts the Nazi war machine is dependent upon.**

It is interesting to note that ports and shipping targets were given priority over industrial targets, echoing the views of the Prime Minister who considered that the 'Battle of the Atlantic' was the most critical battle of the war.

Chapter 6

'Unsurpassed in the Annals of the Royal Air Force'

(JULY TO DECEMBER 1942)

The second half of the year was a rather significant time for the Suffolk airfields. In August the county bade farewell to the doughty Blenheims and their brave crews and then, in November, the faithful Wellingtons left the Suffolk scene; also, the pre war bomber airfields at Honington and Wattisham were transferred to the U.S.A.A.F. In September the popular Commander of No 3 Group, Jack Baldwin, also departed from the scene. Several famous bomber squadrons arrived and one old resident, No 9, left, as did the Canadians of No 419 Squadron. By August No 3 Group had expanded to fourteen front-line squadrons, a total that it would not surpass for the rest of the war. In September a new bomber airfield opened for operations at Chedburgh but towards the end of the year Mildenhall closed whilst concrete runways were constructed. But the highlight of the year came in late November when an airman serving at a Suffolk airfield was awarded a posthumous Victoria Cross for 'his devotion to duty' which was described as 'unsurpassed in the annals of the Royal Air Force'.

'The standard post-operation breakfast of bacon and eggs and a strong mug of char'.
The tension can still be seen on these airmen's faces. (via J. Adams).

The months of July and August proved to be costly for the Command; in total, over three hundred and twenty-five aircraft were lost in action with an average casualty rate of 5.4%, although several operations greatly exceeded this average loss. The steady loss of aircrews began to sap the morale of surviving crews. One airman recalled that 'the joy of successfully surviving a mission over Germany was tempered by the sure knowledge that some of our friends would be missing and we had to face those empty chairs and tables in the mess for the standard post-operation meal of bacon and eggs and a strong mug of char ... followed by bed and hopefully some sleep and not relive the frightening experiences we'd just endured or to dwell upon the thought that it might be our turn next to go for a Burton [literally 'gone for a beer' or 'missing']'. By the time news filtered back to the stations that certain airmen had survived as prisoners of war, most of the personnel had changed and few of the names and faces were remembered.

During July all five Suffolk bomber squadrons suffered losses, some more so than others. No 214 at Stradishall lost its Squadron Commander, Wing Commander K.D. Knocke, over Bremen on 2nd/3rd, when he had been in charge of the Squadron for barely two months. But it was on the two heavy operations to Hamburg towards the end of the month that the Command and No 3 Group suffered heavy losses. On 26/27th when Command Headquarters called for 'a full maximum effort', twenty-nine out of four hundred and three aircraft were lost (7.2%) but only one had flown from a Suffolk airfield – it came from the luckless No 214 Squadron.

Two nights later Hamburg was again the target but because of bad weather over the airfields in northern England, only No 3 Group's squadrons along with ninety operational training crews were despatched and as the weather worsened the latter crews were recalled. Out of the one hundred and sixty-five Stirlings and Wellingtons of the Group, twenty-five failed to return (15.2%). No 9 Squadron from Honington lost three Wellington IIIs and No 419 Squadron also lost a Wellington III. It was believed to have come down in the North Sea as the last message received from the crew was 'Fighters ... wounded ... 500 ft ...' from a position west of the Frisian Islands. The aircraft was captained by Wing Commander John Fulton, D.S.O., D.F.C., A.F.C.; both the D.S.O. and A.F.C. had been awarded during his time at Mildenhall. Also on board was Flight Sergeant H.J. Dell, R.C.A.F., who had already completed thirty operations and had volunteered for just one more sortie. He had previously served in Squadron Leader Turner's crew. The loss of their Commander was deeply felt by the crews and such was the high esteem they held for him that it was decided that his nickname 'Moose' should be added to the Squadron's title; this became permanent when the Squadron's badge was officially authorised by H.M. King George VI in June 1944. It was said that

Wing Commander John 'Moose' Fulton, D.S.O., D.F.C., A.F.C., the Commander of No 419 Squadron R.C.A.F., was killed in July 1942. (via S.L. McDonald)

Fulton had 'inspired a spirit and feeling of confidence which people found unforgettable'. With his passing, the Command (and the R.A.F.) had lost a fine airman and leader. It was extremely difficult to replace commanders of the calibre of John Fulton.

August was a month of change in many respects. On the 7th, No 9 Squadron left the Suffolk scene on its transfer to No 5 Group when its crews would convert to Lancasters. During nearly three years of operations it had mounted almost two hundred and eighty missions for the loss of sixty-six Wellingtons (2.8%) – a more than respectable figure considering the Command's losses over that period. The airfield at Honington would now be occupied by the U.S.A.A.F. and the first American personnel moved in during September.

The other Suffolk bomber airfield to be transferred to the U.S.A.A.F., Wattisham, also closed during the month. No 18 Squadron flew its last Blenheim missions on 17/18th August when eight Blenheim crews attacked airfields at Rheine, Trente and Vechla and all returned safely. This was the final Blenheim operation in Bomber Command and very appropriately Wattisham had also mounted the first Blenheim bombing raid of the war. Four hundred and forty-two Blenheims had been lost by Bomber Command whilst flying over twelve thousand, two hundred and ten sorties (3.62%), which proved to be highest loss rate of the eight major bombers. On the last day of July the Squadron had lost its Commander, Wing Commander C.H. Jones, D.F.C., on a raid to Venlo airfield in Holland. Later in the year the Squadron, still equipped with Blenheims, moved to Tunisia and its new Commander, acting Wing Commander H.G. Malcolm, was awarded a posthumous Victoria Cross

---

No 75 (NZ) Squadron – 'AA' – brought its Wellingtons to R.A.F. Mildenhall in mid-August 1942.

A Stirling pilot ready for take-off.

for his actions that culminated in his death on 4th December.

The Canadian squadron, No 419 (Moose), left Mildenhall on 13th August for R.A.F. Leeming in Yorkshire where it would re-equip with Handley Page Halifaxes and became part of the newly formed No 6 (R.C.A.F.) Group. Two days later another Commonwealth squadron, No 75 (NZ), brought its Wellingtons from R.A.F. Feltwell. Back in April 1940 the Squadron had been transferred to the R.N.Z.A.F. and was then the first Commonwealth squadron to be formed in Bomber Command. Earlier in the month yet another Wellington squadron had arrived in Suffolk when No 101 Squadron arrived at Stradishall from nearby Bourn.

The two new squadrons, along with the older residents, were in action during the month when many familiar German targets – Essen, Duisburg, Osnabrück, Düsseldorf and Mainz – were bombed, but it was two operations on successive nights from 27th to 29th that proved to be particularly costly.

A navigator at his station on a Stirling. Note the 'Pencil Box'! (via J. Adams)

The first operation to Kassel resulted in a loss rate of 10% (thirty-one aircraft) of which two belonged to No 101 Squadron. One of the air gunners lost this night, Flight Lieutenant C.L. Clack, was thirty-four years old, which was quite old for aircrew duties; furthermore it was quite unusual for an airman of his rank to be an air gunner. He had volunteered for flying duties under the 'commissioned air gunners' scheme', which had been introduced in April 1940. Both Nos 75 and 214 Squadrons lost an aircraft on this operation.

The following night, 28/29th, Nuremberg was the target for nearly one hundred and sixty crews. Because of its pre-war Nazi rallies, Nuremberg was considered 'the Holy Grail of the Nazi Party' and it was always high on the Command's list of priority targets. Twenty-three aircraft (14.5%) were lost on this operation, mainly to night fighters, but of the forty-one Wellingtons engaged, no less than fourteen were shot down – a harrowing 34%! Two of these came from No 75 (NZ) Squadron and one of the crews comprised five Flight Sergeants, which not only shows what an experienced crew it was but was also quite rare at this stage of the war. No 101 Squadron lost another two crews and No 149 Squadron at Lakenheath lost its Squadron Commander, Wing Commander C. Charlton-Jones, who had joined the Squadron in May. This 'bastion of Nazism' would continue to take a heavy toll of the Command's crews both in 1943 and 1944.

There were now five bomber squadrons operating from the four Suffolk bomber airfields and the losses continued during September – another twenty-two aircraft and one hundred and twenty airmen failed to return. On 14th September, No 3 Group lost its Commander, Jack Baldwin, the last of the pre-war Commanders to be replaced. In the New Year he was knighted and he remained in the Service until the end of the war. His replacement, Air Vice-Marshal the Hon. Ralph Cochrane, had scant operational experience; since 1936 he had been the Chief of the Air Staff to the R.N.Z.A.F. During his short time in charge of the Group (he left in February 1943) Cochrane never gained the popularity of his predecessor; he was said to be 'a difficult man to get along with' and he appeared to be 'rather austere and humourless'.

Stirling R9358 'BU-A The Saint' of No 214 Squadron at Stradishall; it crashed during take-off at R.A.F. Chedburgh on 9th March 1943 and burst into flames.
(via J.R. Smith)

Cochrane had a forthright manner and demanded a high standard of perfection from his squadrons; he did, however, have the full confidence of Air Marshal Sir Arthur Harris, who called him 'a most brilliant, enthusiastic and hard working leader of men', which was perhaps manifested by his command of No 5 Group right up to the end of the war.

A new bomber station opened at Chedburgh on 7th September. It was sited to the west of the village on the A143 road and about six miles from Bury St Edmunds. The airfield was planned as a satellite to Stradishall but would not become operational until 1st October when the Stirlings of No 214 Squadron moved in from the parent station. The reason for this move was that Stradishall ceased to be an operational station with the formation there of No 1675 Heavy Conversion Flight. These H.C.U.s were the last stage of the operational training of crews. It was no wonder that Air Marshal Harris maintained that 'the education of a bomber crew was the most expensive in the world; it cost some £10,000 for each airman, enough to send ten men to Oxford or Cambridge for three years'!

Yet another Wellington III squadron moved into Mildenhall in the last week of September – No 115 Squadron; it had been in action from Marham since October 1939 but perhaps its main claim to fame was that during August 1941 its crews had made the first operational trials of *Gee*. In the six weeks it remained at Mildenhall before returning to Norfolk (East Wretham)

Stirling N6103 'OJ-E' of No 149 Squadron. The Squadron moved to R.A.F. Lakenheath in April 1942. (R.A.F. Museum)

the Squadron had the misfortune to lose nine aircraft in action; in fact it ended the year with the most unenviable record of the highest losses of aircraft in the whole of the Group – a total of sixty-five Wellingtons.

In the late autumn it was perhaps with some relief for the hard-pressed crews that the Command had been directed to turn its attention to Italian targets; this was to support the Eighth Army's imminent offensive at El Alamein and the planned Allied invasion of North-West Africa – Operation *Torch*, which took place on 8th November. Although these operations were long and very arduous flights (about one thousand, four hundred miles and nine/ten flying hours) they were considered easier operations as the Italian flak was

Flight Sergeant Rawdon H. Middleton, V.C., R.A.A.F.

considerably lighter and less accurate than that experienced over Germany and therefore their chances of survival were far higher. This belief is certainly borne out by the fact that in the fifteen operations mounted to Genoa, Milan and Turin from 22nd/23rd October to 11/12th December when one thousand and eight hundred sorties were flown, the loss rate was 2%. Perhaps the most difficult problems to be encountered were negotiating the Alps both to and from the targets, sometimes in damaged aircraft, and the shortage of fuel, as they were close to the limit of the operational ranges of the Stirlings and Wellingtons.

Turin and its large Fiat motor factories were targeted on seven nights and the raid of 28/29th November led to the posthumous award of a Victoria Cross to one airman of No 149 Squadron flying from Lakenheath – Flight Sergeant Rawdon H. Middleton, R.A.A.F. Born in New South Wales in 1916, he joined the R.A.A.F. in October 1940 and was posted to No 149 Squadron in February 1942. By November he was one of their most experienced pilots, having already completed twenty-eight operations. In August he and his crew had been transferred to No 7 Squadron at Oakington to join the P.F.F., but after their successful return from Nuremberg later in the month he was informed that if he and his crew wished to continue in the P.F.F. he should change his navigator, who was not considered up to the exacting standard required. Middleton refused to break up the crew and so they returned to their old squadron.

On the night of 28/29th seven Stirling crews of No 149 Squadron left Lakenheath for Turin; several, including Flight Sergeant Middleton's crew, had been on a similar operation only eight nights earlier. Because of the severe weather conditions encountered over the Alps only four of the crews carried on to Turin. Middleton, on arrival over the target, made no less than three bombing runs over Turin in order to identify the precise target area. It was whilst the aircraft was on its third run that it was struck by flak and fragments of a shell struck Middleton in one leg, his chest and face, destroying his right eye. He lost consciousness and the aircraft plunged down to 800 ft before being righted by the second pilot, Flight Sergeant L.A. Hyder, who had also been badly injured. The aircraft was hit again and at this stage Middleton regained consciousness and insisted on taking control of the aircraft despite his dreadful injuries.

The Stirling was in a sorry state, there were gaping holes in the fuselage and the windscreen was completely shattered. With supreme skill and unbounded courage Middleton managed to coax his aircraft across the Alps but over France it was again struck by flak. The front gunner, Sergeant J.W. Mackie, who was on his thirty-third mission, was at Middleton's side to give him visual aid and just after two o'clock in the morning the aircraft crossed the French coast. The crew had been airborne for almost eight hours – a long nightmare. By the time the Kent coast was in sight, there was about five minutes of fuel left and because of his injuries, besides those of his co-pilot and the state of the aircraft, Middleton knew that an emergency landing was impossible. He deliberately turned over the English Channel and ordered his crew to bale out whilst he flew parallel to the coast, in order to give them the best chance of survival. Five airmen baled out, including Flight Sergeant Hyder, and all were later rescued from the sea. Mackie and Sergeant J.J. Jeffrey, the Flight Engineer, stayed with Middleton up to the last possible moment; they baled out but did not survive. Just before three o'clock the fuel was exhausted and the Stirling crashed into the sea.

On 13th January 1943 Middleton was awarded a posthumous Victoria Cross and the unusually long and detailed citation ended:

> [He] was determined to attack the target regardless of the consequences and not allow his crew to fall into enemy hands. While all the crew

displayed heroism of a high order, the urge to do so came from Flight Sergeant Middleton, whose fortitude and strength of will made possible the completion of the mission. His devotion to duty in the face of overwhelming odds is unsurpassed in the annals of the Royal Air Force.

It was not until 1st February 1943 that Middleton's body was washed ashore near Dover and four days later he was buried with full military honours at St John's churchyard at Beck Row, Mildenhall but at the rank of Pilot Officer; the news of his commission had not reached him before his death. The five surviving crewmen were awarded the D.F.C. and D.F.M. respectively.

At the beginning of November Mildenhall was closed for operational flying whilst concrete runways were being laid and No 115 Squadron left for Norfolk after a rather short but costly stay. The Squadron would go on to have one of the finest operational records in Bomber Command and sadly be the only squadron to lose over two hundred aircraft in the war. No 75 (NZ) Squadron moved into Newmarket Heath, though at the time most of its crews were at R.A.F. Oakington where they were converting from Wellingtons to Stirlings.

The poor weather that had bedevilled the Command's operations since late September continued through December, but nevertheless operations still continued though with only a relatively small number of crews being involved. An example of these operations occurred on 17/18th when twenty-seven Lancaster crews were detailed to bomb eight small German towns and twenty-eight Stirlings and Wellingtons of No 3 Group were sent to the Opel motor works at Fallersleben; due to the weather conditions only three crews claimed to have bombed the target. Seventeen aircraft (35%) were lost on this night with the Group losing eight crews. The heaviest loss was suffered by No 75 (NZ) Squadron, with only one of its five Stirlings returning to Newmarket Heath. The Squadron Commander, Wing Commander V. Mitchell, D.F.C., was amongst the twenty-nine airmen missing in action; he had been with the Squadron since July. As an illustration of the harsh times experienced by the Group during 1942, No 75 (NZ) Squadron had lost twenty-two aircraft and one hundred and twenty-two airmen in the relatively brief time it had been operating from Suffolk airfields; furthermore, only nineteen of these airmen had survived as prisoners of war but amongst this number was one of the most celebrated escapees - Pilot Officer Eric E. Williams.

He had been the bomb aimer and Captain of one of the Stirlings that failed to return from Fallersleben. It was quite rare for a crew member, other than the pilot, to be the Captain. Williams and his six crewmen were captured, one of whom – Sergeant W.J.S. Voice, R.N.Z.A.F., the rear gunner – was celebrating his twenty-first birthday on that day and was said to have carried with him on the operation a large slice of his birthday cake! In July 1943 Williams was involved in one of the most spectacular and audacious escapes of the Second World War. He and two others managed to tunnel their way out of the East Compound of *Stalag Luft III* (of 'Great Escape' fame) with the help of a hollow vaulting horse – the now celebrated 'Wooden Horse'. It was one of the few occasions during the war in which all who made their escape arrived back in England. Williams was awarded the Military Cross when he finally returned. His best-selling book *The Wooden Horse* was published in 1949, followed in the next year by the equally successful film of the same name, which really set the pattern for subsequent World War escape films.

It is rather interesting to note that earlier in the year (April) the British Red Cross published a small illustrated booklet entitled *Prisoner of War,* which for the first time gave the British public an authentic view of the life and daily regime of the prisoners, as well as the living conditions and also their food rations in the thirty POW camps in Germany. The regular weekly Red Cross parcels – one a week per man – were a godsend for the prisoners; over four hundred tons of foods were being sent to the camps monthly.

The much beloved 'Wimpys' were slowly being phased out of the Main Force despite the fact that in the 'thousand bomber' raid at the end of May there had been more Wellingtons in action than any other bomber. In July No 3 Group had seven Wellington squadrons but by the end of the year the Group was left with just one – No 115.

In the previous three and more years a countless number of Wellington crews had failed to return to their Suffolk airfields. The first two had

Prisoner of War booklet published by the British Red Cross in April 1942.

been lost on 3rd/4th September 1939 and the last Wellingtons to be lost in action by a squadron based in Suffolk occurred on 29th October. 1942. Six Wellingtons of No 115 Squadron, then based at Mildenhall, left on a daylight operation to Essen, and only three returned; fifteen airmen 'lost without trace'. These losses drew to a close a rather glorious chapter of

Bomber Command's operations in Suffolk, a time when its Wellington squadrons had spearheaded the Command's bombing offensive.

As the year came to an end the Command counted the cost of its operations and it would be rather superfluous to say that the losses of aircraft and airmen were the highest of the war so far. But one disturbing feature was the loss of so many experienced Squadron and Flight Commanders, one hundred and twenty-six senior airmen, including three Group Captains; in Suffolk alone seven Squadron Commanders had been killed in action. Such losses had deprived the Command (and the R.A.F.) of very experienced and potentially great Commanders, both for the later stages of the war and the subsequent peacetime years. Air Marshal Sir Arthur Harris remained undaunted; he saw the year as a 'time of preparation' for what he considered was to be 'Bomber Command's main offensive' which would come with a vengeance in 1943.

A Wellington crew about to board their aircraft. The much beloved 'Wimpys' were slowly being phased out of the Main Force.

Chapter 7

The Battle of the Ruhr

(JANUARY TO JUNE 1943)

The year 1943 proved to be the apogee of Bomber Command's long and harrowing war. It witnessed the heavy and sustained offensive against industrial targets in the Ruhr, swiftly followed by the devastating raids on Hamburg, and then in late August the 'Battle of Berlin' commenced. The year was also notable for two spectacular and celebrated operations – the Dams raid in mid-May followed three months later by the attack on the Rocket Research establishment at Peenemünde. Two new and significant electronic guidance aids, *Oboe* and *H2S*, were introduced, which greatly improved target marking and bombing accuracy.

Oboe was really a variation of a system of wireless beams, which had been successfully used by the *Luftwaffe* during their night raids of 1940/1. It was a blind-bombing aid based on pulses transmitted from two ground stations about one hundred miles apart. The aircraft followed a continuous signal from one station (the 'Cat') and the target markers and/or bombs were released at the exact point of intersection from the signal received from the second ground station (the 'Mouse'). There were some limitations to the system – its range was less than three hundred miles and the stations could only cope with six *Oboe*-equipped aircraft in an hour. It was decided to equip the Pathfinder Force's Mosquitos as their operational ceiling of 30,000 ft extended the range to the Ruhr and their superior speed reduced

H2S Mk IIB installation (left) by the navigator's station on a Lancaster.
(via C. Fairlie)

the time over the target area when the *Oboe* aircraft were most vulnerable.

On the other hand *H2S* was an airborne radar system that could transmit a shadowy image of the ground passing below the aircraft, onto a cathode ray (or Plan Position Indicator) carried on the aircraft. Although Command Headquarters claimed 'the problem of accurate navigation under almost any weather conditions is solved by *H2S*', this was a touch of hyperbole. Nevertheless *H2S* proved to be a rather effective aid to both navigation and blind bombing, but it was not the complete answer. Unfortunately within months the Germans managed to develop a system to track the *H2S* emissions and they produced a homing device – *Naxos* – which was fitted to their night fighters.

Although Air Marshal Harris was eager to start his 'main offensive' he was frustrated in this respect by a Directive issued to the Command on the first day of the New Year. He was ordered to attack four French Atlantic ports, which housed the dreaded and dangerous U-boats. Lorient and St Nazaire were considered the main targets with Lorient being selected for 'the heaviest scale of bombing'. From mid-January to mid-February Lorient was attacked on eight nights; over eighteen hundred crews were involved and some four thousand tons of bombs fell on the hapless town and port. It was almost completely destroyed and virtually deserted; according to German sources 'not a cat or dog is left alive'. Unfortunately, the U-boat pens had escaped virtually unscathed; they had been protected by several feet of reinforced concrete and were impervious to the heaviest bombs. Perhaps the only consolation for Bomber Command was that the losses had been slight – twenty-four aircraft in total (a 'mere' 1.3%). Three of these missing aircraft had come from Suffolk squadrons; one from No 75 (NZ) at Newmarket Heath and two from No 214 Squadron at Chedburgh.

These were two of the three operational squadrons operating in Suffolk; the other, No 149, was still at Lakenheath. This situation would prevail for the first three and a half months of the year and it was in fact the least number operating in the county throughout the war. Furthermore, because these squadrons (and others in No 3 Group) were exchanging their 'old'

A familiar wartime photograph – members of No 75 (NZ) Squadron at R.A.F. Newmarket Heath.

Mark I Stirlings for the new Mark III versions, there was a significant reduction in the amount of action for much of this time.

The Stirling IIIs were powered by Bristol Hercules VI or XVI engines, which provided a moderate improvement in speed and operational ceiling as

The cockpit of a Stirling. (via M.C. Ross)

well as slightly better defensive armament. As factory production of heavy bombers had gathered pace, by April each squadron was increased to three Flights, which gave a complement of twenty-four aircraft with another three in reserve. During this time of transition there was a change of Group Commander; on 27th February Air Vice-Marshal Richard Harrison, C.B., C.B.E., D.F.C., A.F.C., arrived and he was destined to remain in command of the Group until July 1946. At the time of his appointment, his Group was the smallest in the Command – just seven operational Stirling squadrons and the two Special Duties squadrons, the latter only nominally under his control.

However, within days (1st/2nd March), Harrison was able to provide sixty Stirlings for an operation to Berlin. Despite the U-boat Directive Air Marshal Harris had already mounted two operations to this 'ultimate target' in mid-January - the first time Berlin had been bombed for fourteen months, well before Harris had taken charge of the Command. For most of these Stirling crews this would be the first time they had been sent to Berlin and although the name looked good in their logbooks, for the kudos it gave them, they would soon come to dread Berlin missions. The flight was long, arduous and physically and mentally demanding; they could be in the air for nine hours or more and most of this time they would be over enemy territory. The intense cold was another physical hazard, let along facing hundreds of searchlights, formidable and intense flak and the inevitable night fighters; Berlin was recognised as the heaviest defended target in Germany. If they survived all these ordeals, they were then faced with a long return flight home across an inhospitable North Sea, frequently in a damaged aircraft and with injured crewmen on board.

On this Berlin operation five Stirlings were lost (8.3%) but the overall loss on the night was 5.6%; the higher losses suffered by the Stirling squadrons, not only over Berlin, would become a serious concern for Command Headquarters in the months ahead. Two more Berlin operations were mounted towards the end of the month – 27/28th and 29/30th – and in the three operations No 149 Squadron lost two crews, which included a most experienced pilot, Flight Lieutenant R.E. Richman, D.F.M., whose medal had been awarded back in June 1941 when he was flying Handley Page Hampdens. No 214 Squadron lost three aircraft and on the last Berlin raid one of the pilots, Flying Officer N.G. Cooper, was the only fatality when his aircraft collided in mid-air with another of the Squadron's Stirlings over Hadleigh on their return to Chedburgh. Flying Officer Cooper was on his first operation of his second tour; all his crew escaped and the other Stirling landed safely.

A Short Stirling being 'bombed up'.

Air Marshal Harris had now decided that his Command was in a position to make a serious and heavy assault on industrial targets in the Ruhr Valley and it was he who called it the 'Battle of the Ruhr'. The Battle commenced on 5/6th March and needless to say it was Essen that was selected as the first target, as it would be on another five nights. In a matter of five months over eighteen thousand, four hundred bombers dropped some thirty-five thousand tons of bombs. It was an awesome demonstration of the power of Bomber Command and large areas of the Ruhr Valley were laid to waste and much of its industrial complex lay in ruins. Without doubt the Battle of the Ruhr was a major victory for Bomber Command and for Air Chief Marshal Harris (he had been promoted in April).

It is interesting to note that in his book *Bomber Offensive* Harris accepted that the Battle was 'an impressive victory' but he did appreciate that:

> It could only be the beginning of a serious bombing offensive, not before a very large number of cities elsewhere in Germany had been reduced to the same condition, and not before the wrecked cities of the Ruhr and elsewhere had been attacked once or even twice again to prevent recovery, could there be any decisive effect.

Photographs taken over the aiming points were always of great interest to ground crews.

An Air/Sea Rescue launch throwing a line to a crews' dinghy.

The Stirling squadrons of No 3 Group were not involved in all the Ruhr operations; but nevertheless, in eighteen raids almost sixteen hundred crews were engaged for the loss of one hundred and seven aircraft (6.7%). This figure was higher than the *average* loss of the Battle, which was just under 5% and was just about sustainable, especially as the operations to other targets during the same period – Nuremberg, Stettin, Turin, Pilsen, Munich and Cologne no less than four times – resulted in lower losses.

The operation to Essen on 5/6th March was a milestone for Bomber Command; not only did it open the Battle of the Ruhr but it was the first major attack on a German target by means of *Oboe*. As Air Chief Marshal Harris later recalled: 'this was the precise moment when Bomber Command's main offensive began'. During the Essen raid the Command also flew its one hundred thousandth sortie. Furthermore it was the most successful of the previous twenty raids on this city: the Krupps factories suffered heavy damage and crews reported a 'solid circle of fire that looked like an immense pot boiling over', the glow said to be visible from at least one hundred and fifty miles. Also the losses were relatively light (at least compared with other Ruhr raids) and only three of the fifty-two Stirlings taking part were lost. Twenty-five crews had left from the three Suffolk airfields and just one failed to return – a Stirling from No 214 Squadron was shot down by flak over Holland and all seven crewmen were killed; it was the first Mark III lost by the Squadron. It would be another month before the Stirling crews were in action again over the Ruhr.

One of the crews' greatest fears was 'ditching' in the sea and escape drills were regularly practised as were the 'ditching positions' to be taken in an emergency. Many felt that 'it wouldn't happen to them' and in truth, considering the numbers of aircraft crossing the North Sea, it was not a common occurrence, although during 1943 the incidence of 'ditching' did increase. Many airmen put it firmly at the back of their minds as they felt that the chances of survival were rather slim. Nevertheless, the Air/Sea Rescue Service with its fleet of fast motor-boats and Supermarine Walrus amphibians rescued over three thousand, seven hundred airmen from the sea, fully justifying its motto 'The Sea Shall Not Have Them'.

On 10/11th April a Stirling III of No 75 (NZ) Squadron had been hit by flak over Frankfurt and then was further damaged by enemy fighters. By now the aircraft was so low on fuel that the pilot, Flight Sergeant G. Rothschild, decided to ditch about three miles off the Sussex coast. The accepted theory was 'tail in first, then the nose' and the Stirling remained afloat for almost twenty-five minutes, ample time for the crew in their yellow life-jackets ('Mae Wests') to get into their inflatable dinghy. Their distress signals had brought a Walrus onto the scene; when it alighted its wash overturned the dinghy but all the crew were safely rescued again, the whole rescue operation taking forty minutes. Amongst the crew were twin Canadian brothers, Robert and Richard Tod, one the wireless operator and the other an air gunner. Sadly both would be killed later in the war, as in fact was the pilot, Flight Sergeant G.K. Sampson, R.N.Z.A.F.

Another Stirling crew, this time from No XV Squadron, was fortunate to be rescued on 24/25th June on return from Wuppertal. The aircraft crashed into the sea about fifteen miles from the Suffolk coast and within two hours they were picked up by an ASR launch from Felixstowe. The pilot, Sergeant N. Towse and Sergeant H.J. Fawley were awarded D.F.M.s for their 'great tenacity'. Later in the year there were another two successful rescues of Suffolk crews but unfortunately there were a greater number of crews who were 'presumed lost at sea'.

In April Mildenhall opened again as an operational station; it had been provided with concrete runways, Drem approach lighting and a new control tower. It was now known as 'Base 32' with 'sub-stations' at Lakenheath and Newmarket. This new system had been introduced mainly because the number of new airfields opening had placed a strain on the Groups' Headquarters. The main 'Base' airfield was normally a permanent pre-war station, which would undertake all the personnel functions of the stations and their squadrons as well as much of the repair and overhaul of the aircraft; the system also facilitated the movement of aircraft between squadrons. The Base Commander was normally an Air Commodore and at Mildenhall, the Commander was no stranger to the Suffolk scene – Air Commodore Andrew 'Square' McKee, D.S.O., D.F.C., A.F.C. He was a New Zealander and at the outbreak of the war he had been a Flight Commander in No 99 Squadron before commanding No 9 Squadron at Honington from January to July 1940. McKee retired from the R.A.F. in 1959 at the rank of Air Marshal and then returned to New Zealand where he died in 1988 aged eighty seven years. Happily many senior officers of the wartime R.A.F. seemed to enjoy a long retirement!

The badge of No XV Squadron, which arrived at R.A.F. Mildenhall in April 1943.

The first bomber squadron to be posted to the refurbished Mildenhall arrived on 15th April and it was one of the most celebrated and oldest squadrons in the Service – No 15, better known as 'XV', the Roman numerals appearing on its badge along with the motto 'Aim Sure'. The Squadron's origins dated back to March 1915 and it was unofficially known as 'Oxford's Own'. The Squadron had already flown Battles, Blenheims and Wellingtons in action but it was now equipped with Stirling IIIs.

Despite all the upheaval of the move, eighteen crews of the Squadron were available for the operation to Mannheim on 16/17th April only a day after their move from Bourn, Cambridgeshire. Although Mannheim was in the Ruhr, the operation was in fact a diversionary raid for the Main Force bound for the Skoda factory at Pilsen. Nevertheless, over two hundred and seventy crews were in action over Mannheim, of which ninety-five were flying Stirlings. The P.F.F. marked the target accurately and the operation was said to be 'very effective'.

Both operations had been conducted in the light of a full moon and

A Messerschmitt Bf 109G 'Gustav' – a formidable night fighter equipped with two MG 151/20 cannons, known as the 'Bomber killer'.

although the clear conditions aided the bombing accuracy, they were also ideal for the enemy night fighters. One of No 214 Squadron's crews bravely and doggedly fought off repeated fighter attacks on their return and Sergeant Hartwell, despite being injured, managed to crash-land his stricken aircraft at Chedburgh; the rest of the crew survived unharmed. Not so lucky was one of his colleagues. Flying Officer D.E. Jones' Stirling crashed in France after being attacked by three Bf 109s. However, four of the crew managed to evade capture and two were captured; only the rear gunner, Sergeant E.M. Lee, had been killed in the fighter attack. One of the successful evaders, Sergeant W.G. Grove, was killed on a Berlin operation in March 1944; he was then a Flight Lieutenant serving with No XV Squadron. One of No XV's Stirlings returned to Mildenhall with three hundred holes in its fuselage and wings, evidence of its battle with the enemy fighters, and one of the gunners, Sergeant Gaylor, was credited with the destruction of a Bf 109.

The night had been very costly for the Command with a total of fifty-four aircraft missing in action (8.9%), which was its highest loss on a single night so far. Once again the Stirling force suffered the heaviest losses – eight (7.3%) – with two crews from both Nos XV and 75 (NZ) Squadrons. As the Battle of the Ruhr continued the Group's losses would increase in severity.

As one airman recalled:

> Raids over the Ruhr were the worst. The towns were so close together that they just passed you from one group of defences to the next. We considered ourselves lucky if we made the target and then back home.

The Air Ministry issued a daily bulletin, which gave details of the Command's previous night's operations and it normally closed with the bland statement that 'last night mines were laid in enemy waters'. This rather terse phrase was almost added as an afterthought and hardly conveyed the rigours and dangers of these operations. But on the morning of 26th April such words masked what had been a disastrous night for the Command and in particular one squadron – No 75 (NZ).

On that night over two hundred crews had been engaged on 'Gardening' operations mainly over the Baltic Sea and around Heligoland; it was the largest mine-laying operation of the war when five hundred and ninety-two

A Stirling being loaded with a mine

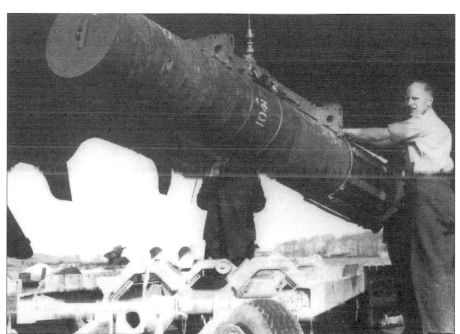

mines had been 'sown' but it also brought the heaviest loss of the war on such operations – twenty-two crews missing (10.6%). Largely as a result of the Command's marked increase in mine-laying, the German *Kriegemarine* flak vessels had been greatly strengthened in those vulnerable areas and they took a heavy toll on this night. Thirty-two Stirling crews were in action and seven were lost, of which four were from No 75 (NZ) Squadron – twenty-eight airmen 'missing at sea'. There was perhaps a small consolation for the Command when it was reported on 2nd May that the elusive *Gneisenau* had sunk in the Baltic Sea after striking a mine. The vessel was now serving as a troop carrier and was bound for Russia. Towards the end of the year mine-laying increasingly became the 'bread and butter' of many Stirling squadrons.

Also during April there had been another costly operation for the Group. On 20th/21st eighty-six Stirlings were sent to attack the Heinkel factory at Rostock, but a most effective smoke-screen concealed the target and the subsequent bombing was very scattered. Eight (10%) aircraft failed to return of which three crashed in Denmark (one each from Nos XV, 75 (NZ) and 149 Squadrons) on their return flights; and No 218 Squadron lost an aircraft on the night.

The hectic pace of operations certainly eased during May; there were

A Stirling III of No XV Squadron – 'LS-P' – crash-landed in Denmark on 20th/21st April whilst returning from Rostock. The crew set their aircraft on fire before being taken prisoners of war.

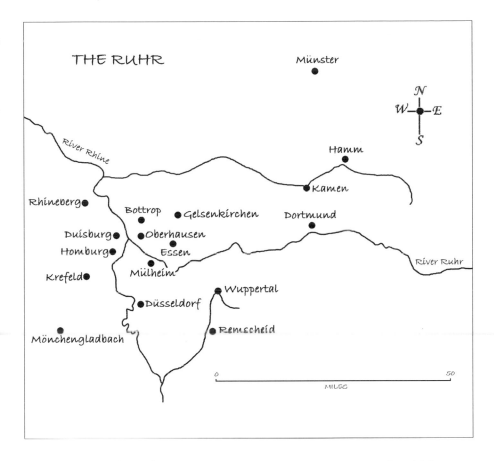

twenty-two nights when no major operations were mounted, which must have been a great relief for the hard-pressed crews. There was a nine-day break in the middle of the month because of the period of a full moon and many crews were given a week's leave, which in theory, if not in practice, was granted every six weeks. Many felt that it was very difficult to return to operations after a week away with families and friends. Over sixty years later one veteran airman clearly recalled this time when he experienced 'acute embarrassment at the praise that was showered on me whenever I left my home' and 'the number of beers I had to politely refuse!' He thought that all this acclaim was due to the celebrated Dambusters raid (16/17th May), which had received widespread coverage in the newspapers.

Despite all the days (and nights) of inactivity, targets in the Ruhr were attacked on eight nights during the month and some of them were the most

A heavily damaged Stirling III of No 75 (NZ) Squadron after returning from the Ruhr. (via J. Adams)

successful of the Battle. The Stirling crews were engaged on six nights and the first to Dortmund on 4/5th was a devastating onslaught which inflicted heavy damage mainly caused by fire; the majority of the Stirling's bomb load was made up of incendiaries. The Command returned to Dortmund on 23rd/24th with over eight hundred and twenty aircraft which attacked in three waves; it was the greatest number involved in a 'non-thousand' raid and the largest operation in the Battle of the Ruhr. The operation was classed by Command Headquarters as 'an outstanding success' and even the German High Command was forced to admit that 'it was probably the worst ever directed at a German city'. It was also the first time that the Group had managed to exceed one hundred Stirlings in action, six of which were lost. Five of these came from the Suffolk squadrons with No 214 losing three aircraft; all but two of the missing twenty-one airmen were Sergeants and their average age was said to be twenty-one years. One of the missing officers was Pilot Officer P.H. Liddle, one of the relatively few South Africans flying in the Command.

After this successful operation Air Chief Marshal Harris sent a personal message to all the squadrons involved:

> Yes, in 1939, Goering promised that not a single bomb would reach the Ruhr. Congratulations on delivering the first 100,000 tons on Germany. The next 100,000, if he wants them, will be even bigger and better bombs delivered even more accurately and in a much shorter time.

Another Ruhr city, Düsseldorf, was attacked two nights later and on 29/30th Wuppertal was the target for seven hundred and ten crews. The damage that was inflicted was thought to be over one thousand acres or about 80% of the built-up area and this raid was considered the outstanding success of the whole Battle. Wuppertal then comprised two towns, Barmen and Elberfield, which had amalgamated in 1929. On this night Barmen had been virtually flattened and Elberfield would receive similar treatment in late June. Eight Stirlings were lost on this operation, with No 75 (NZ) bearing the brunt of the casualties; four crews failed to return to Newmarket Heath and seventeen of the missing airmen were of the R.N.Z.A.F. The only other casualty from a Suffolk airfield was a crew of No 149 Squadron; the pilot, Pilot Officer A.N. Flack, R.N.Z.A.F., was thirty-nine years old, which was far above the average age of most bomber pilots. Although there had been a certain satisfaction at No 3 Group Headquarters that on the last three Ruhr raids the Group had managed to despatch over one hundred Stirlings each night, Air Vice-Marshal Harrison and his Staff officers were concerned that the Group's squadrons were suffering proportionally higher losses than the other Groups. In May the figure had been 6.3% compared with an overall average loss of 4.7%.

The first ten days of June was a time of peace and relative tranquillity at the bomber stations throughout the land and not a single major operation was mounted until 11/12th when Dusseldorf was the target; the previous raid almost three weeks earlier had been one of the few failures of the Battle. On this night the Command achieved another record, over eight hundred and eighty aircraft in action, which was then the highest 'non-thousand' total. Out of this massive armada some seven hundred and eighty crews were bound for Düsseldorf and over seventy crews of the Pathfinder Force for Münster. The Düsseldorf raid went well, it was estimated that one hundred and thirty acres of the city had been destroyed; in fact it proved to be the most damaging raid on the city of the whole of the war. However, thirty-eight aircraft were lost but for a change the Stirlings escaped with light casualties, just two crews, one from No XV Squadron and the other from No 75 (NZ); both were all-Sergeant crews and one crew was on its first operation.

The casualty records for this operation reveal that of the missing two hundred and seventy airmen, 81% were Sergeants and half of the missing aircraft had all-Sergeant crews. Moreover the majority of these crews had completed less than six operations. Thus to all intents and purposes the Command's main offensive was now being waged by young and inexperienced Sergeants, many of them fresh from operational and conversion training; although with the hectic pace of operations they would soon become experienced, that is if they managed to survive long enough. Of course it was a far different matter in the P.F.F. where the proportion of officers was far higher, as indeed was the operational experience of the crews.

There were several significant changes during the latter weeks of the month. On 17th June a new squadron had formed at Chedburgh from 'C' Flight of No 214 Squadron. It was given number 620, and was equipped

---

Widespread damage in Dortmund sustained as a result of the Command's raids in May.

with Stirling IIIs and placed under the command of Wing Commander D.H. Lay; it would soon enter the fray. Three days later another bomber squadron arrived at Lakenheath, No 199, which hitherto had been flying Wellington Xs from Ingham in Leicestershire. Its crews began to convert to Stirling IIIs but it would take them a little longer before they became operational. Then on 26th June No 75 (NZ) Squadron left Newmarket Heath for a new airfield at Mepal in Cambridgeshire. During its stay at Newmarket Heath it had mounted over five hundred and fifty operational sorties for the loss of twenty Stirlings. By the end of the war it had established a very fine operational record, carrying out the fourth highest number of bombing raids, but in the process it suffered the second highest number of aircraft lost – one hundred and ninety-three.

The end of the month was in sharp contrast to the beginning; on six nights from 21st to 26th four targets in the Ruhr – Krefeld, Mülheim, Wuppertal and Gelsenkirchen – were attacked in some strength, followed swiftly by a shattering raid on Cologne. On these six nights No 3 Group lost thirty-six Stirlings, a loss rate of 8%, which was a serious concern not only for the Group but also for Command Headquarters. The heaviest losses were borne by Nos XV, 75 (NZ) and 214, XV with seven crews missing and the other two squadrons each with six. Even No 149 Squadron at Lakenheath, which had established a most enviable reputation for the lowest losses in the Group, had three crews missing from the Cologne raid on 28/29th; during the whole of 1943 the Squadron would only lose three crews on a single night on two occasions, which was quite remarkable considering the level of losses of the other Stirling squadrons. To emphasise the point about the youthful makeup of the Command's crews, one of the missing airmen, Sergeant R.A. Cooper, was only seventeen years old and is thought to be the youngest airman killed in the Command during 1943. Amongst the missing airmen in these three crews were five New Zealanders, two Canadians, one American (although serving with the R.C.A.F.), one Australian and one from the West Indies; such was the cosmopolitan nature of the Command at this stage of the war.

Chapter 8

The Sad Demise of the Stirling

(JULY TO DECEMBER 1943)

The second half of 1943 saw Bomber Command deliver some of its most successful operations of the war, the brief but destructive Battle of Hamburg, the Peenemünde raid and the start of the long and harrowing Battle of Berlin. It also proved to be a time of destiny for No 3 Group and its Stirling squadrons – before the year's end, Stirlings had been withdrawn from targets in Germany.

Perhaps one of the more chilling statistics of the Command's war was that over 17% of its airmen (almost eight thousand, two hundred) were killed in flying and ground accidents, many whilst conducting air tests of aircraft and on training exercises with fighter aircraft. During 1943 No 3 Group lost forty-six aircraft in accidents not directly connected with operations. The most tragic incident occurred on 2nd July over Sudbury, Suffolk, when two Stirlings of No 620 Squadron collided in mid-air whilst engaged on a 'fighter affiliation exercise'; they were avoiding a mock attack by a Bristol Beaufighter. Both Stirlings crashed with fifteen airmen killed and two injured. One of the fatalities was AC1 A. Haigh, who was an air mechanic and only eighteen years old. Later in the year (9th October) a similarly distressing accident happened to a Stirling of No 90 Squadron; it collided with a Hurricane and the Stirling crashed near Mildenhall, killing all nine airmen. One of the aircraft's propellers was placed in St John's Church at

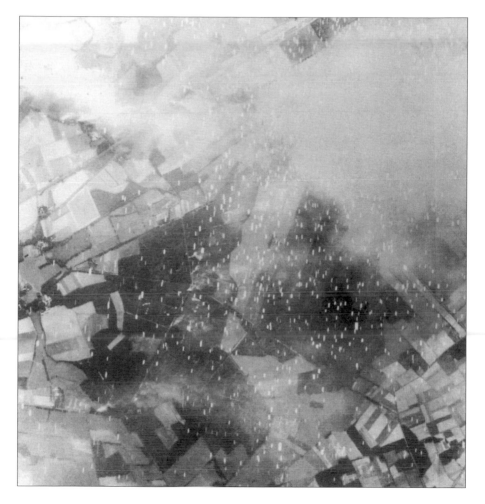

'Window' being dropped over a Ruhr target. It was used for the first time over Hamburg on 24/25th July 1943

Beck Row, where a memorial tablet listing the nine airmen was dedicated on 6th May 1944.

Even whilst the Battle of the Ruhr was still being waged, Air Chief Marshal Harris and his Staff were busy planning a major assault on Hamburg. The city had been his original choice for the first 'thousand bomber' raid but because of an unfavourable weather forecast it escaped the ordeal. Harris had always considered Hamburg to be a major target; it was the

Mk IX Course Setting bombsight on a Stirling. (via J. Adams)

second-largest city in Germany, and also its largest port as well as being an important shipbuilding centre especially for U-boats. During July there were several high-level meetings at Command Headquarters about the Hamburg operation, which had been given a somewhat macabre codename – *Gomorrah*. The city was beyond the range of *Oboe* but it was considered that because of its position on an estuary it would be particularly easy to identify by *H2S* because the outline of water gave a clear response on the *H2S* screen. A tentative date was set for 23rd/24th July.

Cologne was attacked early in the month (3rd/4th) and for the next week the Stirling crews were engaged in mine-laying before taking part in a relatively small raid to Aachen, which actually proved to be most destructive, and which the Germans described as 'a *Terrorangriffen* on the most severe scale';

added to which only one of the fifty-four Stirlings was lost. There was now a welcome break for the crews; for ten nights not a single operation was mounted. Many airmen felt that these long breaks from operations were the hardest to bear: 'the waiting gave us time to think about our lives and our futures, because we knew that as night follows day we would be soon back on the treadmill of operations ... it was almost like seeing ominous black clouds on the horizon coming closer and closer ...'.

Operation *Gomorrah* started on the planned night when almost eight hundred aircraft (including one hundred and twenty-five Stirlings) set off for Hamburg in a continuous stream almost two hundred miles long. The distance from the English coast was about four hundred and fifty miles, which should have taken just over two hours. Two-thirds of the Stirlings' bombload comprised 4 lb incendiaries enclosed in S.B.C.s (Special Bomb Containers); during the Battle of the Ruhr the Stirling squadrons had become known as 'The Fire Raisers'. For the first time *Window* was used – this was bundles of thin metal strips which were designed to confuse the German radar. A bundle of *Window* was released every minute by each aircraft both

---

Hamburg in 1945; one of the most heavily damaged German cities.
(via R. Matthews)

on the way out and the way back. It was a night when 'Bomber Command got everything right'. In a mere fifty minutes, over two thousand, two hundred tons of bombs rained down and *Window* had the desired effect as only twelve aircraft were shot down, the lightest loss on a major operation for over eighteen months. The four Suffolk squadrons were in action, as they would be on the other three Hamburg raids; on this night only No 214 Squadron lost an aircraft to a night fighter. Pilot Officer R.W. Belsher and his crew were on their sixteenth operation and only two survived as prisoners; for some unaccountable reason Belsher's award of the D.F.M. was not made until July 1944.

Because of the quite obvious advantages of *Window*, Essen was attacked the following night for the sixth time during the Battle of the Ruhr. This raid resulted in severe damage to the Krupps factories and the city suffered heavier damage in one night than in all the other raids put together. The overall losses were quite high, twenty-six aircraft, but sadly the Stirling squadrons' losses were proportionally higher (6.7%) with No 620 Squadron bearing the brunt – three Stirlings missing along with twenty-one airmen.

The most destructive Hamburg raid came on 27/28th, when over two thousand, five hundred and twenty tons of bombs were dropped, which brought about the first man-made 'firestorm' and resulted in heavy damage and a large number of civilian casualties. It was after this raid that over one million people fled the city and did not return. Two nights later Hamburg suffered further damage, when it was estimated that six thousand, two hundred acres were destroyed or maybe 74% of the city – Hamburg had been virtually obliterated. It is now considered that the Battle of Hamburg was Bomber Command's greatest victory of the war.

On the following night (30th/31st) Harris brought his long Battle of the Ruhr to a close with a shattering attack on Remscheid, which was situated on the southern edge of the Ruhr and had hitherto escaped bombing. A relatively small force of two hundred and twenty-three aircraft (eighty-seven Stirlings) dropped over eight hundred tons of bombs and over 83% of the town was destroyed. Out of the fifteen aircraft lost, eight were Stirlings (10%); two of these failed to return to Mildenhall and both were from No XV Squadron. On board one of the Stirlings was Lieutenant A.R. Ingle, D.F.C., S.A.A.F.; he was flying 'as a passenger' and is believed to have been the first S.A.A.F. airman to be killed in Bomber Command. Two of No 620 Squadron's Stirlings were lost but all but two of the crewmen survived as prisoners.

The heavier losses sustained by Stirling squadrons, particularly during the Battle of the Ruhr, had caused no little concern at Command Headquarters. The future of the Stirling as a front-line bomber was now in doubt. Harris had written to the Air Ministry: 'The Stirling Group [No 3 Group] has now virtually collapsed. They make no worthwhile contribution to our war effort in return for the overheads'. A high-level conference of Air Ministry officials and the Command's hierarchy was held on 30th July (before the outcome of the Remscheid operation was known). Even setting aside the higher operational losses, the disadvantages of the Stirling were fully discussed and debated. The aircraft had a lower operational ceiling and was thus more vulnerable to enemy flak; also it never gained the full protective cover of the bomber stream. The Stirling carried a lighter bomb load than the Halifax and Lancaster as well as having a restricted mixture of bombs. Furthermore it was considered that with the Mark III, the Stirling had reached the limit of its development, unlike the Halifax and Lancaster. The future operational use of the Stirling was fully debated – as a transport, a glider-tug, or maybe they could be used on 'special duties', effectively dropping supplies to Resistance forces; another use might be maritime and weather reconnaissance duties. However, one thing was decided: the Stirling squadrons of No 3 Group would all be re-equipped with Lancasters with a planned completion date of the spring of 1944.

The Group already had one Lancaster squadron, No 115, which had received Mark IIs in March. This Mark was powered by Hercules engines instead of Merlins; they were built by Armstrong Whitworth and there was a rather limited rate of production. The target date was never achieved partly because of production problems but mainly because of the high losses of Lancasters during the winter of 1943/4; therefore the Stirling continued as an outright bomber for longer than had been planned.

Whilst all this furious debate was raging on the future of the Stirling, the crews were quite happy with their aircraft, as one crewman recalled:

> We on the Stirling squadrons were always made to feel that we were the only ones that mattered – the Rolls-Royce squadrons – as opposed to the mass produced ranks of Lancs and Hallies...

Wing Commander Mike Wyatt, D.F.C., the Commander of No 75 (NZ) Squadron, who had flown Stirlings with No XV Squadron in late 1942, thought that 'it was a very nice aeroplane to fly', but he did admit that 'flying below the Lancasters and Halifaxes was an uncomfortable experience'! Nonetheless, the losses of Stirlings in the coming months would seriously test the crews' confidence and faith in their aircraft.

August was the most active month of the year for the Command's crews and the Stirling squadrons were engaged in nine major operations; rather swiftly their losses began to escalate. The month opened with the fourth raid on Hamburg, which because of severe thunderstorms proved to be the least successful and remarkably No 3 Group had the lowest losses. On the 10th, 'C' Flight of No XV Squadron became the core of a new squadron at Mildenhall – No 622; its Commander was Wing Commander G.H.N. Gibson, not to be confused with his more illustrious namesake, Guy Gibson of Dambusters fame. The new Squadron was immediately in action with five crews engaged over Nuremberg and all returned safely.

Air Chief Marshal Harris had to bow to political pressure to direct his Force to Italian targets in an attempt to hasten Italy's departure from the war. Six operations were mounted to Genoa, Milan and Turin from 7th to 16th, all completed with relatively light losses. On the raid to Turin on 12/13th a Stirling pilot of No 218 Squadron, Flight Sergeant Arthur A. Aaron, D.F.M., was awarded a posthumous Victoria Cross – shades of Rawdon Middleton. Aaron was only twenty-one years old and on his nineteenth operation. Three nights later Turin was again bombed and it proved to be the last raid on targets in Italy; the first had been back in June 1940. Italy surrendered in early September.

Without question the most impressive and successful operation of the month was *Hydra* – the attack on the V2 Rocket Research establishment at Peenemünde on the Baltic coast. This was the first time that the Command had attempted a *major* precision raid at night on such a small target. It was also the first time that one pilot called 'Master of Ceremonies', or 'Master Bomber', controlled the whole operation by radio. The importance of this operation was impressed on the crews at their briefings: 'If you don't knock out this target tonight, it will be laid on again tomorrow and every night until the job is done'. As one airman recalled many years later, 'that was the first and only time we had been told that, so we knew it was an important target'.

Almost six hundred aircraft left for Peenemünde, of which just fifty-four were Stirlings. The operation was deliberately conducted in bright moonlight so as to improve the chance of success, and the bombing would be conducted at 8,000 ft, so for a change the Stirling crews were not at a disadvantage. In a matter of an hour some one thousand, eight hundred tons of bombs were dropped and much of the research station and the workers' accommodation were destroyed. It was a spectacular success, probably the pinnacle of the Command's achievements throughout the year. Although forty-three aircraft were lost (6.7%) only two Stirlings failed to return, one each from Nos XV and 620 Squadrons.

Winston Churchill was eager for Bomber Command to resume its attacks on Berlin. The last major raid had been almost five months ago and since then the Command had inflicted heavy damage on targets in the Ruhr and,

The workers' housing area and the V2 Rocket Assembly Hall at Peenemünde after the remarkable raid.

Groundcrews enjoying a break for tea whilst loading bombs at R.A.F. Lakenheath in late 1943. (Imperial War Museum)

of course, Hamburg. The Prime Minister now felt that the same treatment should be visited on the German capital. It would appear that Harris felt it was a little early to make an all-out assault on Berlin because he later maintained that the 'Battle of Berlin', as it became known, began on the night of November 18/19th. Harris responded to the call and on 23rd August he ordered 'a maximum effort' and as a result over seven hundred and twenty crews were briefed. The briefings were held in the late afternoon and one airman of No 214 Squadron at Chedburgh recalled, 'Morale was so good, despite our losses getting higher, that there was a great roar of joy at having a crack at the Big City'. Wing Commander Desmond McGlinn, the Squadron's Commander later remembered that, 'It was not fully dark when we crossed the coast [of Holland] on the way in. It was a beautiful night; one could almost see Berlin from the coast'. Most of the Stirling squadrons had taken off between 20.30 and 21.00 hours.

For a variety of reasons only three-quarters of the crews actually reached Berlin, but out of the one hundred and twenty-four Stirling crews a higher percentage (88%) actually bombed. The operation was only partially successful and much of the bombing fell short of the target area. The crews faced fierce opposition from both flak and a strong night fighter force believed to number over two hundred and

Loading mines on a Stirling of No 199 Squadron at R.A.F. Lakenheath.

fifty. The loss of fifty-six aircraft was the highest so far on a single night and sixteen of them were Stirlings – 13% of the crews that set out or almost 15% of those that reached Berlin. Every one of the six Suffolk squadrons involved lost at least one crew – eight in total, which was half of the Group's total losses. Amongst the seventy-two airmen missing in action, two of No 214's crews were on their twenty-fourth operation and one pilot of No 620 Squadron, Pilot Officer G W M McDonald, was on his thirtieth operation. Both Nos 199 and 622 Squadrons lost their first Stirling IIIs in action. One of No 199 Squadron's aircraft was shot down shortly after completing its bomb run and the rear gunner, Sergeant A N Nixon, recalled:

> We had bombed and had nearly got to the edge of the searchlight area, we thought we were over the worst. Then it was as though a giant hand took hold of us and there was a huge shuddering and shaking sensation, just like a massive dog shaking a rat ... The next thing I knew was that I was coming down on the end of a parachute ...

Sergeant Nixon was the only survivor of the crew; he was taken prisoner of war.

Four nights later (27/28th) eleven Stirling crews failed to return from

Nuremberg before one hundred and six Stirlings were in action over Berlin on 31st August/1st September and once again the Stirling squadrons suffered the highest casualties – seventeen (16%) – with No 214 Squadron losing three crews. After this heavy raid over 1½ million women and children were evacuated from Berlin. In the two Berlin operations No 3 Group had lost thirty-three Stirlings and Harris decided to withdraw the Stirling and Halifax squadrons (which had also suffered higher losses than the Lancasters) from the next Berlin operation which was scheduled for 3rd/4th September.

Nevertheless, the Stirling crews were still engaged on seven major operations during September, twice to Mannheim and Hannover. The first Mannheim raid was an example of Bomber Command performing at its peak; the P.F.F. marking was almost perfect and the city suffered severe damage but eight Stirlings were lost, three from No 149 Squadron, only the second time in the year that it had suffered so. When Hannover was the target on 22nd/23rd, it had escaped a heavy raid from Bomber Command for almost two years but three nights later it was attacked again and on this night each of the six Suffolk squadrons lost a crew out of a total of ten lost (9%). Probably as a result of the mounting losses No 3 Group's squadrons were omitted from the two further Hannover operations mounted in October. In fact, this month proved to be a quiet time for the Group and its Stirling crews. This was quite remarkable as the Group then had its highest number of operational Stirlings on its complement – one hundred and eighty-four. It was obvious that the days of the Stirling as a Main Force bomber were now severely numbered.

In October a new bomber airfield opened at Tuddenham; it had been constructed to the east of the village. The first operational squadron to use the new airfield was No 90, which arrived from Wratting Common, Cambridgeshire, on the 16th. Needless to say, it was equipped with Stirling IIIs and at long last the Squadron had found a permanent home where it would remain for the rest of the war. Prior to this move the Squadron had experienced a rather peripatetic war with Tuddenham becoming its eighth wartime station. It had also been the only squadron in Bomber Command to be equipped with Boeing Fortress Is for bombing operations, which had proved to be a less than successful experiment to say the least. Earlier in the month (7th) two crews of No 214 Squadron initiated the dropping of supplies to Resistance forces in France, augmenting the work of the Group's two 'Special Duties' squadrons Nos 138 and 161.

It was towards the end of November that the fate of the Stirling as a front-line bomber was sealed. On 18/19th Mannheim and Ludwigshafen were the targets for almost four hundred aircraft of which one hundred and fourteen were Stirlings. The operation was really a diversionary raid in support of four hundred Lancasters bound for Berlin. In that respect it certainly achieved its desired objective because only 2% of the Lancasters were lost, whereas twenty-five aircraft on the diversionary mission were shot down, mainly by night fighters; nine of them were Stirlings (7.9%). Although there was heavy cloud over the target area, it was judged that the Daimler Benz motor factory had been heavily damaged; certainly Mannheim was not seriously bombed again until March 1945. On the night, No 622 Squadron lost two crews with Nos 149 and XV Squadrons each losing one aircraft; this happened to be the last Stirling that No XV Squadron lost in action. Since April 1941 the Squadron had lost one hundred and thirty-four Stirlings, the highest number of any Stirling squadron. The crews were

Three unknown members of a Stirling crew on return from Berlin, 22nd/23rd November 1943. Five out of fifty Stirlings were lost and it was the last time that Stirlings attacked Berlin.

now screened from any further bombing operations whilst they converted to Lancasters.

The Stirlings were rather unceremoniously withdrawn from German targets directly following the operation to Berlin on 22nd/23rd. Of the seven hundred and sixty-four crews taking part, just fifty were flying Stirlings; this was the largest force the Command had despatched to Berlin. Although there was heavy cloud cover over the city, the marking and bombing were accurate and it was the most successful Berlin operation so far. Five Stirlings were lost (10%), one from No 622 Squadron and one from No 214 Squadron. This was the last Stirling the latter Squadron lost on bombing operations; in fact the crew never reached Berlin. On the outward flight one of its engines was put out of action by enemy flak to the east of Hannover and the pilot, Flight Sergeant G.A. Atkinson, decided to return to Chedburgh, but over Holland it was further damaged by an attack from a night fighter. Although the Stirling survived the attack, the loss of power and severe icing meant that it

A Stirling crew being debriefed after their Berlin operation of 22nd/23rd November 1943. (via J. Adams)

Stirling IIIs of No 90 Squadron arrived at R.A.F. Tuddenham in October 1943.
(Imperial War Museum)

was continually losing height as it crossed the North Sea and the pilot saw no alternative than to ditch the aircraft, which he successfully managed. Sadly he and the rear gunner, Sergeant W. Sweeney, failed to escape from the aircraft; after several hours afloat the other five crewmen were rescued by an ASR launch.

When Command Headquarters analysed this latest Berlin raid, the statistics revealed that the Stirling losses were close to 13%, but with the number of crews that had aborted their missions the 'real' loss rate was closer to 16%. Furthermore, since August No 3 Group had lost one hundred and nine Stirlings over Germany. Faced with such figures Air Chief Marshal Harris felt that he had little alternative but to withdraw the Stirlings from targets in Germany. He later said that he 'could not countenance the depletion of so many squadrons and their brave airmen'. Thus at a stroke of the pen Harris and his Main Force had lost eleven squadrons.

Within days of this decision No 620 Squadron left Chedburgh for Leicester East to serve in Transport Command, where its Stirlings would operate as glider-tugs. No 214 Squadron also left the airfield for Downham Market, Norfolk from where it would serve in the newly formed No 100 Group of Bomber Command. Chedburgh, like Stradishall, now became mainly engaged in crew conversion training, which left just three operational

A Lancaster taking-off with 'FIDO' in operation. (via T. Murphy)

bomber stations in Suffolk – Lakenheath, Mildenhall and Tuddenham – and only three 'effective' Stirling squadrons: Nos 90, 149 and 199.

Maybe it was because it was being phased out as a front-line bomber that Dame Laura Knight, R.A., an official war artist, used a Stirling as the model for her painting, *Take Off, Interior of Bomber Aircraft*; one of No XV Squadron's aircraft was set aside for her at Mildenhall as her 'studio'. The now famous painting is on display in the Imperial War Museum but it was first exhibited at the Royal Academy in 1944. The wireless operator who features prominently in the foreground of the painting was Flight Sergeant Roy Escreet, D.F.M., of No XV Squadron; he was later killed in action in March 1945 at the rank of Flight Lieutenant.

In November another new airfield opened in Suffolk at Sutton Heath, about four miles to the south-east of Woodbridge. It was of rather special construction and known as an 'Emergency Landing Ground', being provided with a massive concrete runway three thousand yards long and two hundred and fifty yards wide, and was for the specific use of damaged aircraft for emergency landings. To the bomber crews it was more commonly known as

The famous painting by Dame Laura Knight, R.A. A Bomber crew preparing for take-off. (Imperial War Museum)

the 'Prang or Crash 'drome', or sometimes as 'OZ' from its identification code. Although R.A.F. Woodbridge was never under the control of Bomber Command, it is included here purely because so many of the Command's crews used the airfield when in dire emergencies; over four thousand, one hundred and ten emergency landings were made by Allied bomber crews, thus saving countless lives.

Also during November another important device was used operationally for the first time. 'FIDO' (or more properly 'Fog, Intensive, Dispersal Of'!) was a system of large pipelines laid along each side of a runway into which petrol was injected under pressure and then fired by burners set at intervals along the pipelines; the intense heat thus generated caused an updraught that dispersed the fog in the vicinity of the runway. FIDO was not only instrumental in saving the lives of many bomber crews but also enabled Bomber Command to maintain its operational schedules when weather conditions at the home airfields would have dictated otherwise. FIDO became operational at R.A.F. Woodbridge in June 1944 and later at R.A.F. Tuddenham.

During December the Stirling crews were out 'Gardening' on seven nights and each of the three squadrons lost a crew. The last crew from a Suffolk squadron to be killed in action during 1943 belonged to No 149 Squadron; the seven airmen were 'lost without a trace' on 20th/21st whilst engaged on a mine-laying operation off the Frisian Islands; it is thought that their aircraft was shot down by a night fighter. In many respects this crew was the epitome of the majority of the Command's crews during 1943; it comprised three R.A.F. airmen, two Canadians and two Australians, all were Flight Sergeants or Sergeants and their average age was twenty-one years.

The Command had paid a high price for the heavy damage it had inflicted on German cities and towns and its industrial capacity, with over fifteen thousand, eight hundred and thirty airmen killed and thousands more taken prisoner of war. No 3 Group had lost almost five hundred aircraft in action, the second highest in the Command, and the majority of these were Stirlings. It was a sad time for the Group. Since September 1939 it had been in the forefront of the Command's offensive, but now most of its squadrons would play a relatively minor and secondary role for a considerable time whilst the long and ponderous conversion to Lancasters took place.

Chapter 9

From Berlin to the Normandy Beaches

(JANUARY TO 6TH JUNE 1944)

During December 1943 the crews at Mildenhall had been busy converting to Avro Lancasters. After its operational debut in March 1942 this legendary bomber really epitomised Bomber Command during the last three years of the war. Perhaps the only surprise was the length of time that had elapsed before Lancasters made their appearance in Suffolk.

The Lancaster had come into being almost by accident when its immediate predecessor, the twin-engine Manchester, failed to live up to expectations. The Avro 683 prototype flew on 9th January 1941 and was powered by four Merlin X engines. The Mark I had a maximum speed of about 285 mph and cruised at 210 mph. The Lancaster was originally designed to carry 4,000 lbs of bombs but this figure rose steadily to the 12,000 lb 'Tallboy' and ultimately the massive 22,000 lb 'Grand Slam'; the only Allied bomber capable of carrying these bombs. The Lancaster was a remarkable bomber of which over seven thousand, three hundred and seventy were built and over 46% were lost in action.

Before the Lancaster crews at R.A.F. Mildenhall took their new bombers into action for the first time on 14/15th January, a Lancaster of No XV Squadron had been lost on a training flight on the previous day; it crashed into the Wash after an engine fire and the six airmen were killed. Brunswick was the target for the squadrons' Lancaster crews; it would be the first time

At last Lancasters arrive on the Suffolk scene – two from No XV Squadron in formation. (via R.J. Hall)

that its citizens experienced a major raid and nearly four hundred crews were in action. It was a costly night for the Command with thirty-eight aircraft lost (7.6%) but all the Lancasters arrived back safely to R.A.F. Mildenhall, although a Lancaster of No 622 Squadron crash-landed on return but none of the crew were injured. From now on the crews at Mildenhall would be engaged in a different kind of air war compared with their colleagues in the three Stirling squadrons at Lakenheath and Tuddenham. They would be engaged over Berlin and other major German targets whilst the Stirling crews were sent out on mine-laying, and dropping supplies to the Resistance forces; in fact on one night in January (28/29th) Nos 90 and 199 Squadrons each lost a Stirling whilst engaged in mine-laying over Kiel Bay and all fourteen airmen were killed. These two vastly different types of operations resulted in a fair number of casualties in the months ahead.

However, during January 1944 the Stirling crews returned to bombing operations, albeit rather briefly, when they were briefed for what were known as *Crossbow* operations. In the autumn of 1943 intelligence had revealed that a number of 'construction sites' were being prepared in the Pas de Calais, thought to be for the assembly, storage and launching of 'unmanned bombs'. It was not until the end of November that almost eighty 'ski-sites', as they were called, had been identified as launch sites. It was decided that Bomber Command, along with the American Eighth Air Force, would attempt to locate and destroy them. Air Chief Marshal Harris stipulated that mainly Stirlings would be used for these *Crossbow* operations. Actually they seemed to provide an ideal task for the Stirling squadrons – a relatively short flight, light or lighter fighter opposition and bombing from a low altitude with no other heavy bombers above them. The Stirling force would be led by *Oboe* Mosquitos of the P.F.F. to locate and mark the targets.

The crews' briefings were conducted in high security and they were only told that their targets were 'construction sites of special aeronautical facilities

The cockpit of a Lancaster. (via D. Gower)

of major importance'. The first *Crossbow* operations had been mounted by the Command in December but neither of the raids was successful due to the problems of locating the small targets, which were well hidden in woods. During January over two hundred and sixty Stirling crews were engaged on four nights attacking fifteen sites, of which only four were thought to have been destroyed but only one Stirling was lost. Harris was not happy with the situation and he successfully argued that these operations were better suited to the light/medium bombers of the Second Tactical Air Force and thus his Command was relieved from *Crossbow* operations, at least until mid-June when the first 'unmanned bombs' – V1s or 'flying bombs' – actually landed on south-east England.

The Mildenhall crews' different air war continued with a vengeance on 20th/21st when they were in action over Berlin as the Battle of the 'Big City' intensified; indeed they would return to Berlin on another three nights during January. Then during February they were also engaged in Operation *Argument*, later more popularly known as 'The Big Week'; this was a combined Allied bombing offensive directed at the German aircraft and ball bearings industries. It opened on 19/20th February when the distant target of Leipzig was attacked and the Command suffered its heaviest loss so far – seventy-eight aircraft (9.5%), one of which was a Lancaster of No XV Squadron that failed to return. 'The Big Week' continued with major attacks to Stuggart, Schweinfurt and finally Augsburg on 24/25th. Considering the Command's heavy losses on these operations, it could be said that the two Mildenhall squadrons escaped fairly lightly: No XV lost two Lancasters and No 622 one crew over Schweinfurt.

For most of February and the early weeks of March the Stirling crews were mainly involved in mine-laying and dropping supplies to the Resistance in France and Belgium. With the invasion of Europe only months away, the heavy demand for arms, ammunition and other supplies was beyond the capabilities of the two Special Duties squadrons; No 90 Squadron was especially busy on these operations and subsequently it was temporarily seconded to No 38 Group of Transport Command. These supply drops were not quite the 'milk runs' (easy missions) that most crews had imagined as seven Stirlings of the three Suffolk squadrons were lost during this period with Nos 90 and 199 Squadrons each losing three aircraft.

It must have given the Stirling men some sense of satisfaction when in the middle of March they found themselves back on bombing raids. This was a result of the 'Transportation Plan'; a most ambitious bombing offensive against rail centres, depots, marshalling yards and major junctions in northern France and Belgium, with the objective of creating a 'railway desert' in order to hinder and delay the movement of troop reinforcements and supplies being sent to Normandy after the invasion. Because of the imminence of Operation *Overlord* – the invasion of Europe – the Allied Chiefs of Staff had decided that the time was ripe to activate this Plan. It had been hotly debated at the highest political level on account of the high risk to the civilian population because most of the selected targets were situated in built-up areas; also Air Chief Marshal Harris and his American counterpart both thought that their heavy bomber forces could be better employed over German industrial targets. Harris also harboured some doubts about his Force's ability to accurately mark and bomb such precise targets. Before the final decision was taken he was directed to carry out some trial operations.

Two raids were made by Lancasters early in March before thirty-eight Stirling crews were engaged in a raid on the marshalling yards at Amiens on 15/16th. Two of the Suffolk squadrons each lost a Stirling. One from No 149 Squadron was shot down over the target and all the crew were killed. Perhaps more tragically, a Stirling from No 90 Squadron was almost back home safely when it collided with a Wellington from No 11 Operational Training Unit and both aircraft crashed in Buckinghamshire; all fifteen airmen were killed. The Stirling pilot, Flight Sergeant J.V. Spring, was only eighteen years old, which was very young for a Command pilot even at this stage of the war. The pilot and captain of the Wellington, Flying Officer J.H.S. Lyons, D.F.C., R.A.A.F., was a most experienced airman, who had already completed one operational tour. The following night, Amiens was attacked again and these 'Transportation' targets continued during March with raids on Laon, Auloyne, Courtrai and Vaires but with no further casualties. Air Chief Marshal Harris was surprised with the success of these operations and the Transportation Plan was fully activated with Bomber Command being allocated thirty-seven specific railway targets, over the coming two months. Harris and his Command would devote a considerable amount of resources to the Plan.

During March the two Lancaster squadrons at Mildenhall despatched one hundred and ninety sorties. Stuttgart and Frankfurt both suffered two heavy raids during the month, more especially Frankfurt when on two nights (18/19th and 22nd/23rd) over one thousand, six hundred and sixty crews were in action. The city sustained heavy and extensive damage. As a local report commented, it was 'the most fateful blow of the war ... a blow which simply ended the existence of Frankfurt, which had been built up since the Middle Ages'.

The power and strength of Bomber Command at this stage of the war can be clearly seen in the scale of its operations. For instance on 24/25th when the 'Battle of Berlin' finally came to a merciful conclusion, eight hundred and sixteen crews were involved. It proved to be a tragic operation for the Command with seventy-two aircraft lost (8.9%) and out of the forty-four missing Lancasters, No XV Squadron lost two aircraft. The 'Battle of Berlin' had been a very costly offensive for Bomber Command: six hundred and twenty aircraft had been lost with over three thousand, eight hundred airmen missing in action of whom about 80% were killed; the majority of these airmen are buried in the Berlin War Cemetery. During this long and harrowing offensive, No XV Squadron had taken part in nine raids and had lost seven aircraft (both Stirlings and Lancasters) or 7.3%, whereas No 622 Squadron had lost ten aircraft (8.3%) in the same number of raids. All the

Relaxed crews after returning from Frankfurt on 22nd/23rd March 1944.

Junkers Ju 88G-1 night fighter. They took a heavy toll on the Command's aircraft in early 1944. This aircraft of III/NJG2 landed 'in error' at R.A.F. Woodbridge on 13th July 1944!

crews were agreed that these Berlin missions were the most traumatic of all: 'the worst weather, the coldest conditions, the heaviest flak, the most searchlights, the greatest fighter opposition ... in short, a journey into hell ...'. If ever one of Bomber Command's operations deserved a special campaign medal or star then without doubt it was the 'Battle of Berlin', which had been relentlessly waged by its crews with great determination, strong fortitude and the utmost courage.

Two nights later (26/27th) Essen was the target and despite the city's awesome reputation, 'only' nine aircraft were lost (1.3%), the lowest nightly loss on a major raid for many, many months; it would appear that the sudden switch to a Ruhr target had taken the German air defences by surprise. However, sadly, a crew of No XV Squadron failed to return. After this remarkable 'escape' from such a notorious target, morale in the Command was at a high and more so amongst the almost eight hundred crews that were briefed for Nuremberg on 30th March; but nothing could prepare them for such a terrifying and horrific ordeal. They were well aware that it would be a long and arduous flight, about one thousand, three hundred miles there and back from Suffolk or at least seven hours' flying time. One of their concerns at the briefings was that the operation would be during the full moon period, although the Meteorological officers assured them that high cloud cover was forecast for the outward journey – but the 'Met men' had been proved wrong before!

The twenty-seven crews at Mildenhall (eleven from No XV and sixteen from No 622 Squadron) took off between 22.15 and 23.00 hours. The outward flight was made in bright moonlight (the forecast had been wrong) and several survivors of this operation, sixty-three years later, still shudder when they see a full moon; it brings back memories of that night. For well over one and a half hours on the way to Nuremberg the crews were engaged in an intense and ceaseless battle with the enemy's night fighters and the majority of the aircraft shot down never reached the target. One of No 622's crews was shot down near Frankfurt and all the crew were killed; they were on their twelfth operation. One veteran pilot recalled, 'I still have nightmares about seeing so many Lancasters going down in flames'. By a cruel twist of fate Nuremberg was covered by heavy clouds and there were strong crosswinds which hampered the marking and accurate bombing, with the result that only slight damage was sustained. As one airman remembered:

> To put it politely, the bombing and marking appeared to be a bit of a shambles, which was hardly surprising after what we had gone through on the way to the target.

Furthermore, about one sixth of the crews bombed Schweinfurt, which was some fifty miles to the north-east, by mistake. The return flight by the surviving crews was a little less fraught. However, it was a quite appalling slice of ill-fortune that resulted in the loss of another Lancaster of No 622 Squadron. Over the south-eastern corner of Belgium the Lancaster collided with a Halifax of No 427 Squadron; both aircraft were some fifty miles off course and only one of the fifteen airmen survived the collision.

There was utter disbelief and horror at the Command Headquarters as the cost of the night's operation became apparent: ninety-five aircraft were missing (14%) and another ten crashed on their return to Britain. This would be the heaviest loss suffered by the Command throughout the war. Over five hundred and twenty airmen were killed and more than one hundred and fifty taken prisoners of war; the greatest loss on a single night. Many of those killed on this tragic operation are now buried in the Durnbach War Cemetery, about ten miles east of Bad Tölz in Bavaria. Quite remarkably, nine of the forty-nine squadrons involved in the operation managed to survive the ordeal without losing a crew, and one of these was No XV Squadron. This Nuremberg operation is deeply etched in the annals of Bomber Command.

Durnbach War Cemetery in Bavaria. (The Commonwealth War Graves Commission)

This ill fated raid ended three months of quite horrendous losses for Bomber Command when a total of one thousand, eight hundred and nineteen aircraft had been lost in action, which was equal to at least thirty-five Main Force squadrons. At this casualty rate the Command could not have continued its offensive for very long but for the amazing production rate of replacement Lancasters and Halifaxes and more importantly, the ability of Training Command to produce a constant stream of trained crews to replace the five thousand, seven hundred airmen killed or missing in action during this period.

The railway yards at Chambly, France after the attack on 1st/2nd May 1944.

The five Suffolk squadrons had lost a 'mere' thirty-five aircraft in these three months and two hundred and fifty airmen, of whom twenty-two managed to evade capture and return to fight again. Most of these evaders were shot down over France where the numerous 'escape lines' were now well established. Although it was not a unique occurrence, nevertheless it was very rare when the whole crew of a Lancaster of No XV Squadron managed to evade capture on 15/16th March when they were en route to Stuttgart. To further illustrate the large contribution made by Commonwealth airmen to Bomber Command, no fewer than fifteen pilots (43%) of those missing airmen were serving with either the R.C.A.F., R.A.A.F. or R.N.Z.A.F., as were one fifth of the other crewmen.

In April the overall control of Bomber Command, along with the American Eighth Air Force, passed to General Eisenhower, the Supreme Allied Commander in Europe, although the effective control was vested in Air Chief Marshal Sir Arthur Tedder, his Deputy; he had been instrumental in planning and proposing the Transportation Plan. The actual date of the transfer was the 14th and although Harris was not too enamoured with the situation, he did concede that 'the comparatively brief period was absolutely the only time when I was able to proceed with a campaign without being harassed by confused and conflicting directives'. Nevertheless, when circumstances and weather conditions dictated, Harris was able to mount some attacks on German targets – Cologne, Essen (yet again!), Düsseldorf, Munich, Schweinfurt and Friedrichshafen – and in some respects he could justify these attacks on strategic grounds.

The attack on Friedrichshafen on 27/28th is a good example as the town housed several factories making tank engines and gearboxes. It was a risky but brave decision on his part; the target was deep in southern Germany and the attack was planned to take place in the full moon period – shades of the ill-fated Nuremberg raid less than a month earlier. It proved to be a most effective and successful operation with 67% of the town destroyed. However, it was a little costly: eighteen Lancasters lost (5.6%), two of which came from No XV Squadron along with one from No 622 Squadron. Considering the losses sustained in the first three months of the year, it was remarkable that on several nights during April the Command was able to mount over one thousand, one hundred sorties each night and, moreover, suffer relatively light losses, at least when compared with the earlier months.

During April the now dwindling Stirling squadrons were more active than they had been previously during the year; their crews were engaged on a mixture of Resistance supply drops, mine-laying and bombing railway targets. It was over one of the latter targets – Chambly – on 20th/21st that fourteen Stirlings were equipped with a new blind-bombing aid, *Gee-H* (*G-H*). This bombing aid was reputed to enable the bomber force to bomb accurately in almost any weather conditions. It used *Gee* in conjunction with an airborne transmitter/receiver and two ground stations and beacons. *G-H* had been trialled towards the end of 1943 but its introduction had been delayed until sufficient equipment had been produced. The tail fins of the aircraft equipped with *G-H* were prominently marked with a yellow flash in order that the other aircraft could follow the *G-H* leaders and bomb when they did.

Chambly was situated about eighteen miles due north of Paris and was a major railway repair centre for northern France. Over the following two weeks it would be bombed on another three nights by Lancasters and Stirlings of No 3 Group and the damage inflicted on the centre was considered one of the most successful operations of the Transportation Plan; this target was almost the swansong of the Stirling as a strategic bomber. Several other railway targets were bombed during the month and the Allied Chiefs of Staff still held reservations about the number of civilian casualties, so much so that the Stirling crews of No 149 Squadron visited many towns in Belgium and France to drop leaflets explaining the reasons for the heavy night bombing of railway installations.

Early in 1944 the Air Ministry had decided that a number of airfields would be further developed as 'Very Heavy Bomber Stations' in order to accommodate either the large Boeing B-29 or the R.A.F.'s new heavy bomber that was still on the drawing board with the tentative name 'Windsor'. Thus it was during May that Lakenheath was closed to operational flying; No 199 Squadron had already departed for North Creake, Norfolk and on 14th May No 149 Squadron moved to Methwold, also in Norfolk. The Squadron had been part and parcel of the Suffolk scene since April 1937 and its crews had been in action since the first day of the war; in fact No 149 was one of only two squadrons to serve continuously in Bomber Command throughout the war. The Squadron completed almost seven hundred and forty operations for the loss of one hundred and thirty-one

Stirling crews of No 149 Squadron at R.A.F. Lakenheath. The Squadron left Suffolk in May after seven years.

Both of these Lancasters of No XV Squadron – 'LS-M' and 'LS-Q' – were in action on 5/6th June 1944 and both were lost within ten days of D-Day. (via R.J. Hall)

aircraft (Wellingtons, Stirlings and Lancasters) – one of the finest records in Bomber Command. As for Lakenheath, its wartime existence was over and the airfield would not reopen until July 1948. This closure left just two operational bomber stations in Suffolk – Mildenhall and Tuddenham – and a solitary Stirling squadron, No 90. The Squadron was next in line to be equipped with Lancasters but it was still operating its Stirlings over Normandy on D-Day.

During May No 90 Squadron had the misfortune to lose three Stirlings on Resistance operations, and another was lost on 23rd/24th when it crash landed shortly after take off whilst bound for mine-laying off the Frisian Islands; all seven airmen were killed. The aircraft – BK784 – was a 'veteran' Stirling III which had been with the Squadron for thirteen months and during this time it had completed fifty-four operations, one of only twenty-seven Stirlings to complete over fifty operations.

With Operation *Overlord* only a couple of weeks away, the Command was in action virtually every night; there was little respite for the crews but at this rate their operational tours would be completed in record time, especially as the losses were relatively light. In the last ten nights of May over five thousand, two hundred crews were in action mainly over railway targets and coastal batteries – the latter were situated in the Pas de Calais and these operations were among the many attempts to deceive the enemy about the precise location of the imminent invasion. During this time No 622 Squadron lost three crews over railway targets – Angers and Trappes. One of the pilots taken prisoner on 31st May/1st June on the Trappes operation was First Lieutenant J.A. Braithwaite, U.S.A.A.F.; although not unique it was quite rare for an American airman to be the pilot and captain of a Command crew, three of whom were Canadians.

From 23.30 hours on 5th June to 05.30 hours on D-Day wave upon wave of Lancasters and Halifaxes were in action over Normandy in Operation *Flashlight*. Bomber Command flew over one thousand, three hundred and thirty sorties and dropped some five thousand, two hundred tons of bombs – another record. Heavy cloud cover made accurate bombing a problem. One hundred and six Lancasters of No 3 Group were the tenth and last wave of the armada of heavy bombers and their targets were the coastal batteries and ammunition stores at Ouistreham and those to the north of Caen, which were directly behind one of the five landing areas – *Sword* beach.

Twenty Lancasters of No XV Squadron and fifteen from No 622 Squadron left Mildenhall between 03.00 and 03.45 hours on the 6th. None of the crews were aware that it was D-Day, all they were told was that their targets were the defences along the shores of the D-Day landings. There were several celebrated Lancasters involved on this operation. No XV Squadron had L7566 'LS-Z' which had taken part in the very first Lancaster operation on 3rd March 1942 and also LL806 'LS-J *Jig*', which although it was only flying its fourteenth operation would ultimately complete one hundred and forty. By sheer coincidence No 622 Squadron also had a Lancaster (LL885 'GI-J') named *Jig* – it too was on its fourteenth operation and would survive to complete another one hundred and nine. All thirty-five crews arrived back safely at Mildenhall at about the time that the first ground troops were going ashore – 06.30 hours.

Even the rather maligned Stirlings still had a part to play in this massive air operation. Although No 3 Group was now left with just three Stirling squadrons, twenty-two Stirling crews (including fifteen from No 90 Squadron at Tuddenham) were engaged in Operation *Titantic*: their task was to drop dummy paratroops over Marigny, a couple of miles to the east of St Lô. This was an attempt to make it appear as if real paratroops had landed and the dummies were provided with sound and light simulators to imitate small arms fire. The plan was to divert the enemy's attentions from the actual dropping zones. The *Musee de L'Occupation* at Ste Mére-Eglise in La Manche, Normandy has one

Stirling III 'WP-B' of No 90 Squadron; one of only three Stirling squadrons in No 3 Group. (via J. Adams)

of these dummy paratroops on display in its small museum. Other Stirling squadrons, no longer in Bomber Command, were in action on 5/6th June and on D-Day towing gliders with 'real' paratroopers on board.

The *Official History* was a trifle critical of the Command's performance:

> The unsuitable weather nullified, to a large extent, the advantage enjoyed by the Allies of overwhelming air superiority. This was largely because the heavy bombers could not operate in such conditions.

Nevertheless Operation *Neptune*, the actual assault phase of *Overlord*, was a success and furthermore the Command had lost only eight aircraft – a mere 0.7%. By the evening of 6th June, as the crews set off once again for targets in Normandy, they were well aware that the long-awaited invasion of Europe had taken place and they were all very proud to have played a part in it. In the coming weeks they would be called upon to fly many more operations in support of the Allied ground troops, but surely the end of the war must now be in sight?

Chapter 10

The Resurgence of No 3 Group

(JUNE TO DECEMBER 1944)

With the Allied forces safely, if somewhat tenuously, landed on the narrow strip of Normandy coast, the Command's operations were immediately directed to those rail and road centres that were considered essential for the movement of enemy reinforcements and vital supplies. The crews would be called upon to provide direct battle support as well as bombing ammunition and oil storage depots. However, the first flying-bomb landed on England on 13th June and the crews would be frequently engaged in attacking the launching sites and storage areas, which would be an ongoing campaign for almost two and a half months.

The relatively light losses experienced by the Command and the three Suffolk squadrons in the previous few weeks changed rather dramatically from 7/8th June. On this night four rail centres were the targets for over three hundred and thirty aircraft, of which twenty-five Lancasters left Mildenhall for Massey-Palaiseau, a rail centre about fourteen miles to the south of Paris. Because these targets were further away from the battle front the German night fighters had more time to intercept the bomber force and twenty-eight aircraft were lost (8.3%). It was a harsh night for Mildenhall: six crews failed to return – four from No XV Squadron and two from No 622 Squadron an overall loss of 24%!

One of No XV's missing crews was most experienced. The seven airmen between them had an average of forty operations and they were led by Squadron Leader P.J. Lamason, D.F.C., R.N.Z.A.F., who was the Commander of 'A' Flight. Another of the Squadron's Lancasters survived a furious attack from two Messerschmitt Me 410s and the pilot, Flight Lieutenant W.J. Bell, D.F.C., managed to make a successful emergency landing at Friston airfield in Sussex. The navigator, Sergeant C.W. Kirk, had been killed in the fighter attack but the remainder of the crew escaped with injuries only shortly before the aircraft exploded.

Three nights later when railway targets at Dreux were attacked, No XV Squadron lost another crew and No 90 Squadron lost their first Lancaster in action. A week later No 90 Squadron mounted its last Stirling operation

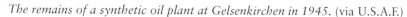

The remains of a synthetic oil plant at Gelsenkirchen in 1945. (via U.S.A.F.)

when a few crews were engaged in mine-laying around the Channel Islands. This proved to be the Squadron's one hundredth 'Gardening' operation. Since the Squadron had been equipped with Stirlings back in November 1942 the crews had flown over two hundred and ten operations and had lost fifty-eight Stirlings in action (3.0%), another example of the higher loss rates suffered by Stirling squadrons.

General Eisenhower had reiterated that the main strategic priority for both Bomber Command and the American Eighth Air Force was the German synthetic oil industry; he had specifically requested that Bomber Command should attack those targets in and around the Ruhr. The first operation in this new oil offensive was mounted on 12/13th and was directed against the Nordstern oil plant at Gelsenkirchen. It was a most successful and devastating operation; over one thousand, five hundred tons of bombs were accurately dropped on the oil plant and production ceased for ten weeks. It was a trifle costly though, with seventeen aircraft missing (6.1%) and each of the Suffolk squadrons lost a crew. From this operation until mid-March 1945 the various oil plants at Gelsenkirchen would be bombed by

H.M. King George VI, Queen Elizabeth and Princess Elizabeth with crews at R.A.F. Mildenhall – 5th July 1944. (R.A.F. Museum)

the Command on another eleven occasions, mainly by *G-H* Lancasters of No 3 Group, besides daylight attacks by the American Eighth Air Force.

The first attack of the new offensive directed on the V1 launching sites was made on 16/17th June and before the month was over No 90 Squadron had lost two crews in action over these targets. One very experienced crew was lost over Rimeaux on 24/25th. The captain and pilot, Warrant Officer E.C. Roberts, D.F.M., was thought to have completed over forty-five operations and had been awarded his D.F.M. in July 1941 whilst flying Handley Page Hampdens with No 50 Squadron. Three nights later two of the Squadron's Lancasters were returning in the early morning of 28th June from bombing a V1 site at Biennais when they were attacked by an enemy intruder, an Me 410. One Lancaster crashed near Icklingham, Suffolk and all the crew were killed, the other Lancaster was damaged as it was making its landing approach to Tuddenham and all but one of the crew survived; the rear gunner, Flight Sergeant P.W. Smith, was killed in the fighter attack. It certainly was no consolation to the Squadron but this was the last time in 1944 that an R.A.F. aircraft would be shot down by enemy intruders.

On 5th July, much to the delight of all the personnel at Mildenhall, H.M. King George VI accompanied by Queen Elizabeth and H.R.H. Princess Elizabeth visited the station. These Royal visits were informal affairs (at the specific request of King George VI) with the officers and airmen on parade wearing normal working battledress and they were greatly appreciated by all the airmen and airwomen who were serving there; they felt that he was 'their King' as he had once served in the R.A.F. and was particularly knowledgeable about the air war. One of the main hangars had been specially decorated for the occasion and thirty airmen were invested with their medals. It was almost nine years to the very day since H.M. George VI (then Duke of York) had visited Mildenhall, but what a change in such a short period of time.

July was notable for two successful and spectacular operations. On 20th/21st the Scholven Buer oil refinery at Homburg was the target for one hundred and forty-seven Lancasters; the plant was thought to provide the *Luftwaffe* with about one thousand tons of aviation fuel daily. The damage inflicted on this night seriously reduced the flow of fuel. Unfortunately, the German night fighters took a heavy toll on the Lancaster force and twenty were shot down (13.6%) – six of these came from the Suffolk squadrons. No 90 Squadron lost three crews and the one Lancaster of No XV Squadron that failed to return was piloted by Flight Lieutenant W.J. Dell, D.F.C., who had only recently escaped from a severe crash landing, quite obviously he

and his crew had used up their ration of good fortune. Also on board was Flight Lieutenant D. C. Evans, who was the Squadron's Engineer Leader; only one airman survived as a prisoner of war. On this operation No 75 (NZ) Squadron, now operating from Mepal, lost seven of its twenty-five aircraft; during the war most bomber squadrons experienced at least one torrid operation when everything appeared to go wrong.

Then, on 24/25th July, Stuttgart was the target, the first of three heavy raids on the city within five nights. These raids caused the heaviest damage that Stuttgart received during the whole of the war. In total over fourteen

A Lancaster crew wait for their aircraft to be prepared for action. (via J. Adams)

hundred crews were involved and seventy-two aircraft were lost; over half of these went missing on the third raid (28/29th). This operation was conducted during the full moon period and the *Luftwaffe* accounted for thirty-nine Lancasters mainly on the outward journey. Considering such a heavy loss the three Suffolk squadrons escaped with light casualties; five in total were lost.

There is a tendency to believe that at this late stage of the war the Command's crews comprised predominantly young airmen, but when the losses from the Suffolk squadrons are analysed, there were a surprising number of airmen in their mid or late thirties. The oldest airman killed over Stuttgart was Flying Officer R.B.V. Harris of No 622 Squadron, who was thirty-nine years old whereas the youngest, Sergeant P.W. Brackley, also serving in the Squadron, was only nineteen.

During August the crews of No 3 Group were in action on eleven days and nine nights. Most of the daylight operations were directed at flying-bomb sites and the final one was mounted on the 28th of the month when twelve launching sites were attacked. A few days later they were captured by the Allied forces; they had finally broken out of Normandy and were streaming across France.

By the middle of the month Air Chief Marshal Harris had decided that the time was ripe to return to Germany with a vengeance, despite the fact that Bomber Command was still nominally under the control of General Eisenhower. Brunswick and Rüsselheim were bombed on 12/13th and on these raids the Command's total tonnage of bombs dropped during the war exceeded five hundred thousand tons. In the last week of the month Stettin, Bremen and Kiel were attacked, as well as second raids directed at Rüsselheim and Stettin. Both could be considered legitimate strategic targets, Rüsselheim, with its large Opel motor factory, and Stettin an important

'Tail-End Charlie' – a Lancaster rear gunner. (via M.R. Smith)

and busy port about one hundred miles north-east of Berlin. Not many of the crews would have had experience of such a long and exhausting flight, probably nine to ten hours in the air. On the second Stettin raid No 90 Squadron lost two aircraft; one crashed in Denmark on the return flight with a total loss of life and the other crashed almost in sight of Tuddenham with the loss of three airmen. Although overall the Command's losses during the month were slight, on daylight operations they were a mere 0.3%. Nevertheless, No 90 Squadron had a relatively costly time with seven crews missing in action compared with two each from the other two Lancaster squadrons.

Many crews had a deep psychological fear of collisions which only deepened as the numbers of aircraft on an operation greatly increased. In truth collisions between 'friendly' aircraft were not a very high risk, at least according to the boffins at Command Headquarters; they considered that a collision with an enemy night fighter was a far greater hazard. But like all statistics they could be proved wrong in most tragic ways as No 622 Squadron found out to its cost in September; in a matter of one week they lost four crews due to collisions with friendly aircraft, no fewer than twenty-nine airmen killed. On 12/13th, whilst engaged over Frankfurt, one of the Squadron's aircraft collided in mid-air with a Lancaster of No 625 Squadron; none of the fourteen airmen survived. Then on 20th September a number of the Squadron's crews were engaged on a formation flying practice and two of the Lancasters collided and crashed about six miles from Colchester, Essex. Only four days earlier (16/17th) one of No 90 Squadron's Lancasters was returning from attacking German flak positions at Moerdijk, prior to Operation *Market Garden* (the airborne landings at Arnhem and Nijmegen) when it collided with a Lancaster of No 115 Squadron and both crews were

Enemy flak batteries were still a force to be reckoned with at this late stage of the war. (Imperial War Museum)

killed. So much for theoretical predictions!

At long last, on 15th September, the reins of Bomber Command were returned to Air Chief Marshal Harris and he was once more free to devote his increasingly stronger bomber force against German industrial targets, impelled by his strong conviction that by doing so he could bring about Germany's downfall. One of several new squadrons that were formed in the autumn was based at Tuddenham. On 5th October 'C' Flight of No 90 Squadron formed the nucleus of a reformed squadron – No 186 – which was placed under the command of Wing Commander J.W. Giles, D.F.C. From April 1943 it had been an Army Co-Operation unit equipped with Hurricanes, then Typhoons and ultimately Spitfires; it was later renumbered 130 as a fighter squadron with the Air Defence of Great Britain. Few squadrons had served in three different commands in such a short space of time, and now it was to be equipped with Lancasters to join the Group's expanding *G-H* Force. However, the crews had to wait a while before they were fully supplied; in fact they 'borrowed' some Lancasters from No 90 Squadron in order to become operational.

September proved to be significant for Bomber Command in two important respects. On the 13th of the month Sir Arthur Harris received the directive for Operation *Hurricane*, which was to be

> …a demonstration to the enemy in Germany generally, the overwhelming superiority of the Allied Air Forces, in this theatre, with the maximum effort directed against objectives in the densely populated Ruhr.

Such an order was 'meat and drink' to the Air Chief Marshal; after all, in early 1942 he had promised them that Germany would 'reap the whirlwind'. With quite remarkable promptitude, on the following day, a devastating attack was mounted on Duisburg, swiftly followed by a night operation to Duisburg and Brunswick. The night operation to Duisburg was sent out in two waves, two hours apart; within the space of twenty-four hours almost two thousand crews were in action dropping over ten thousand tons of bombs, totals that would not be exceeded again in the war. It was a massive demonstration of the strength and power of Bomber Command

A Lancaster of No 218 Squadron 'HA P' leaving R.A.F. Chedburgh.

and mercifully the three operations were conducted at a small cost – twenty-four aircraft – a mere 0.9%. One crew of No 186 Squadron failed to return from the Duisburg night operation. They were flying a Lancaster 'borrowed' from No 90 Squadron, and furthermore they were a very young and inexperienced crew: one member was nineteen years old, two were twenty and three were twenty-one years. In the Squadron's records they are all shown as 'lost without trace' and, like so very many of their colleagues in Bomber Command, their names appear on the fine Runnymede Memorial at Cooper's Hill, Surrey. It was difficult for relatives and friends to accept the loss of such young men, all the more so as they had no known grave.

It is interesting to note in passing that 8th September marked the end of the Stirling as a bomber. It was an 'old' Suffolk squadron – No 149 – that brought the Stirling's bombing career to a close when four left Methwold to join a force of Lancasters and Mosquitos to bomb enemy troop positions at Le Havre; all four aircraft returned safely. Another chapter in the history of

Bomber Command had closed.

In October it was decided to give Air Marshal R. Harrison, the A.O.C. of No 3 Group, almost a free hand in the deployment of his *G-H* Lancaster Force, a decision that proved to be most propitious. The main feature of the *G-H* operations was that they comprised comparatively small numbers of Lancasters operating by day and escorted by fighters, with a remarkably low loss rate. Air Marshal Harrison would ultimately be provided with about eighty *G-H* Lancasters which he spread equally amongst his squadrons.

The first independent *G-H* raid was mounted to Bonn on the 18th of the month; it was an old city that had not previously been bombed, which was probably the reason why Air Marshal Harrison selected it as it would show the effectiveness of the *G-H* operation. It was a complete and utter success with heavy damage inflicted on the city for the loss of one Lancaster. A new and potent bomber force had arrived on the scene; from now until the end of the year No 3 Group launched thirty-two *G-H* operations, all but three by day, for the loss of forty-five Lancasters (1%). Because of the restrictive range of *G-H* and its fighter escort, the *G-H* Force was mainly in action in and around the Ruhr, particularly to oil targets but also to important road and rail communication centres, especially as the Allied land forces advanced towards Germany.

It was probably just and very fitting that No 3 Group made such a resurgence at this late stage of the war. It had largely led the Command's early bombing offensive with its Wellington squadrons before experiencing such a costly and torrid time with its Stirling squadrons.

On 1st November the Command Headquarters received yet another Directive:

> ...to inform you in view of the great contribution which the strategic bomber forces are making by their attacks on the enemy's petroleum industries, it has been directed that the maximum effort is to be made to maintain, and, if possible, intensify pressure on this target system.

Sir Arthur Harris had always considered the bombing of oil refineries and plants as 'panacea targets', which only diverted his Force from 'genuine' industrial targets; he pencilled his comment alongside this order: 'Here we go round the mulberry bush'! However, he was probably unaware that back in 1918 it had been prophesised that, 'Oil has become, in time of war, the blood of victory'.

Nevertheless, despite his misgivings he launched fourteen major raids on oil targets in the Ruhr during November, with four operations directed against the Meerbeck oil plant at Homburg; the last one on the 21st was perhaps the most successful, returning crews reporting 'vast yellow flames followed by thick black clouds rising to a great height'. In the four Homburg operations only fourteen Lancasters were lost (1.8%) but on the second raid two Lancasters of No XV Squadron went missing; they had collided at 20,000 ft and only two of the fourteen airmen survived. One of the pilots, Flight Lieutenant B. Earley, D.F.M., MiD, was a most experienced airman, who was on his forty-fifth operation; he had been awarded his D.F.M. back in August 1942 when flying Wellingtons with No 101 Squadron.

The Squadron suffered another blow on the 16th when the Command was called upon for the first time to provide air support for the American land forces; they were requested to bomb three towns near the German border that were about to be attacked by the American troops. The Squadron's target was Heinsberg, just across the border and about twenty miles north of Aachen. Only one Lancaster out of one hundred and eighty-two was lost – it was piloted by No XV's Squadron Commander, Wing Commander W.D.G. Watkins, D.S.O., D.F.C., D.F.M., and he was the only member of his crew to survive as a prisoner of war. He had been in charge of the Squadron since April and was a most popular Commander, having over fifty operations to his name. There were not that many airmen still flying operationally who had flown since the early years of the war. Watkins had joined the Service in the early 1930s and had originally trained as an observer. He had been awarded his D.F.M. in June 1940. His replacement as Squadron Commander was Wing Commander N.G. McFarlane, D.F.C.

Perhaps the sheer determination and bravery of the Command's crews can be shown by one incident on 27th November when a crew of No 90 Squadron was in action over the Kalk Nord railway yards in Cologne. Their Lancaster was hit by flak over the target area. The pilot, Flying Officer D. Jones, still managed to bomb the target but within minutes the aircraft was struck again which caused severe damage to one of the engines. Turning for home the aircraft, now losing height, was struck by flak on another two occasions. It was clear that they would not make it back so Flying Officer Jones decided to execute a crash-landing near Valenciennes, near the French/ Belgian border. Although having very little control of the aircraft, Jones managed to avoid several trees and nearby houses before crash-landing, quite remarkably all the seven airmen escaped with not a single injury and of course they were rescued as they had landed in Allied-held territory. Although the *Luftwaffe* was not such a potent threat as hitherto, largely on account of an acute shortage of aviation fuel, the enemy's flak batteries still managed to claim a number of the Command's bombers.

On 27/28th November when Neuss, an important supplies centre, was attacked by mainly *G-H* Lancasters, No XV Squadron dropped the relatively new 12,000 lb DP 'Tallboy' bomb. This deep penetration bomb had been first used in June; it was designed to penetrate some 25 ft into the ground before exploding. By the end of the war over eight hundred and fifty 'Tallboys' had been dropped on a variety of targets, such as U-boat and E-boat pens, viaducts and canals.

During November a new Group was formed within Bomber Command – No 7 – which was essentially to co-ordinate and centralise the large programme of heavy conversion training for crews. Thus both Stradishall

A 12,000 lb DP 'Tallboy' bomb shackled into the bomb bay of a Lancaster of No XV Squadron. (R.A.F. Museum)

and Chedburgh relinquished their training commitments and the stations were able once again to return to operational status, increasing the number of the Group's bomber stations based in Suffolk to four – Chedburgh, Mildenhall, Stradishall and Tuddenham.

On 5th December No 218 squadron arrived at Chedburgh from Methwold, Norfolk, making a welcome return to the county after a lapse of four years and four different stations. Since those days 'Gold Coast' had been added to its title, in recognition of its adoption by the people of that Colony in late 1941. In August the Squadron had exchanged its Stirlings for Lancasters and it would now take its place in the Group's *G-H* Force. Stradishall received its operational squadron a little later; just a week before Christmas No 186 Squadron moved in from Tuddenham and would remain at Stradishall for the rest of the war.

During December the Group's *G-H* Force was in action on fourteen days as well as on three nights. Most of its targets were road/rail communications in western Germany, especially those supplying the German offensive in the Ardennes. There was the occasional synthetic oil target, most notably the one thousand-mile flight there and back to Leuna near to the town of Merseburg on 6/7th December; this was the Command's first major raid on an oil target in eastern Germany. Although there was heavy cloud over the target, post-operation photographs revealed considerable damage. Five out of the four hundred and seventy-five Lancasters were lost and one of them belonged to No 186 Squadron. The aircraft was returning and had dropped to an altitude of 8,000 ft to avoid icing when it was struck by lightning, finally crashing near Brussels. All seven airmen baled out but the rear gunner, Flight Sergeant J. Skelton, D.F.M., did not survive. He had already completed one tour with No 207 Squadron. This was just a further example of another additional hazard faced by the crews – weather conditions. The loss rate on this operation was 1.3%, which was about the average for the Command in the latter months of the year; nevertheless there was still the odd day or night operation when the losses were considerably higher.

One such operation came on 12th December when the Ruhrstal steelworks at Witten in the Ruhr was the target for one hundred and forty *G-H* Lancasters. This was the town's first major raid of the war. Enemy fighters engaged the bomber force over the target and eight Lancasters were lost (5.7%); two of them came from No 218 Squadron and only one crew survived. The second Lancaster had been severely damaged by flak and was making its way back to Chedburgh on one engine. However, the pilot, Flight

Lieutenant H. Warwick, realised that it would not make the English coast so he completed a successful ditching in the North Sea about fifty miles from Felixstowe and all the crew were safely rescued. A crew from No XV Squadron also failed to return; it was believed that they had been shot down by flak rather than enemy fighters. Sadly the operation was not successful; the steelworks survived virtually undamaged, because the bombing was very scattered. This was one of the few *G-H* operations that could be rated as a failure.

No 218 Squadron had the misfortune to lose another two crews on the last day of the year when over one hundred and forty *G-H* Lancasters bombed the railway yards at Vohinkel, near Solingen. These attacks were mainly conducted at a relatively low altitude to enhance the bombing accuracy and as such the aircraft were rather vulnerable to enemy flak. The Squadron suffered the only losses on this operation and only one airman survived as a prisoner. Even at this late stage of the war there was a great disparity in the ages of the crew members. One of the missing airmen, a navigator, Sergeant V.T. Phillips, was thirty-eight years old, whereas the tail gunner, Sergeant R. Morley, was only eighteen.

During 1944 No 3 Group had lost a total of four hundred and four heavy bombers in action, of which three hundred and thirty-five were Lancasters. Out of this total, No XV Squadron had lost forty-three with No 622 Squadron losing thirty-eight, quite a number of these aircraft having been lost in the costly Berlin operations early in the year. The only other squadron to serve continually from Suffolk during the year – No 90 – had lost forty-four aircraft, of which twenty-seven were Lancasters. Considering that the Squadron had lost its first Lancaster in mid-June, it had suffered proportionally higher losses during the second half of the year. For some unaccountable reason the Squadron had also acquired an unenviable record: from early August there was not a single survivor from any of its missing crews.

It had been a quite momentous year for Bomber Command, almost reaching the pinnacle of its performance for the whole of its war. The Command had managed to survive the horrendous losses in the early months, and then during the summer its crews gave continuing support to the Allied land forces before returning to German targets both by night and by day, which effectively doubled its efficacy. Large areas of the Ruhr lay in ruins and if truth be told, Bomber Command was running out of viable targets.

During the latter months of the year the number of squadrons and front-

'Lancasters at dusk.' By the close of 1944 there were five Lancaster squadrons operating from Suffolk airfields. (Imperial War Museum)

line aircraft had increased markedly, and the Command would enter its sixth year of the air war as a massive force of quite awesome power. It should not be forgotten that Bomber Command was the only Allied force that had been in action since the first day of the war. Just how much longer would its brave and valiant crews have to venture forth into the skies above Germany?

Chapter 11

'On to Victory and Beyond'

Came the New Year nothing much changed for the crews, it was business as usual. Despite the very poor weather conditions in January 1945, No 3 Group's crews were in action on eight days and six nights. As the weather improved during February the Group's independent *G-H* Force mounted operations on eleven days and two nights as well as joining the Main Force on four night operations, perhaps most notably to Dresden. Most of the *G-H* raids were made to railway yards, oil and Benzol plants in or near the Ruhr. For much of the time these targets were obscured by heavy cloud and the success of these operations speaks volumes for the technical expertise of the crews and the excellence of their equipment.

Overall these *G-H* operations were conducted with almost minimal loss of aircraft, and frequently all the crews engaged on the raids returned safely. As one veteran airman recalled of those early weeks of 1945:

> We had got to a stage of the war when we all *expected* to come back. We joked that we would see each other at the pub in the evening and the first ones there bought the beer! So it was a great shock and a deeper sense of sadness when friends went missing. You see I think we all were aware that the war wouldn't or couldn't last that much longer, but we didn't talk about it, as it didn't do to tempt providence and think too much about the future.

In actual fact, during January, ten crews that had left the four Suffolk airfields failed to return, two being lost on the first night of the year (1st/2nd) when the railway yards at Vohinkel were under attack once again. Both aircraft were struck by 'friendly fire' whilst returning over Belgium. The Lancaster of No XV Squadron made a safe crash-landing in France and all the crew were safe, but the crew from No 218 Squadron were not so fortunate. Their Lancaster had already been damaged by flak at a height of 21,000 ft whilst in the target area and then the 'friendly fire' caused one side of the aircraft to catch fire; only one of the crew survived. Since the Allied occupation of Belgium the threat of 'friendly fire' had become just an additional hazard to be faced when returning from the Ruhr. However, on the positive side, Belgium now proved a 'godsend' for many crews, who were able to land their damaged aircraft on one of the several airfields there.

A small piece of the Command's history was made when the old and faithful 'Wimpy' finally bowed out of Bomber Command on 7/8th January

Lancaster III – LM577 'HA-Q Edith' – of No 218 Squadron at R.A.F. Chedburgh. It finally completed the war with 84 operations to its credit. (via J. Adams)

– a solitary Wellington of No 192 Squadron was despatched over the North Sea 'to investigate enemy beam signals connected with the launching of flying-bombs and believed to emanate from marker buoys'. It must have seemed like an eternity since the first Wellingtons entered the Command with No 99 Squadron at R.A.F. Mildenhall back in October 1938; they were still, of course, being used in Operational Training Units.

Both Nos XV and 218 squadrons suffered losses on 28th January when the Gremburg marshalling yards at Cologne were attacked. Out of the one hundred and fifty-three Lancasters of No 3 Group, three were missing in action – all from Suffolk squadrons. A Lancaster of No XV Squadron was shot down before reaching the target but all eight airmen survived; four of them were Australians. Two from No 218 Squadron were lost to enemy flak near the target and although eight of the fifteen crewmen survived as prisoners of war, amongst those killed was Sergeant E.N.J. Francis, a navigator, who at the age of forty was one of the oldest operational airmen and Warrant Officer J. Towns, D.F.C., a tail gunner, who was flying his final operation and who had already been screened from further operations.

In February No 90 Squadron suffered two severe setbacks in the space of two weeks. On 2nd/3rd when Wiesbaden was the target for the very first time, Wing Commander W.G. Bannister, D.F.C., was leading his crews when, about half an hour after taking off from Tuddenham, there was a minor collision with another of the Squadron's Lancasters. The Wing Commander's Lancaster went out of control, crashed and exploded some three miles from Bury St Edmunds and all eight airmen were killed. The other Lancaster, although damaged, landed safely back at the airfield with no injuries to any of the crew. Wing Commander

Wesel from the air in May 1945 (R A F Museum)

Bannister, along with two of his crew, was buried in St John's churchyard, Beck Row. He was a 'true blue', an ex-territorial Army officer who had entered Cranwell College in 1934 as a Pilot Officer. He had also been a noted athlete and represented Great Britain at the Olympic Games in Berlin in 1936. Bannister had attained the rank of Wing Commander back in March 1941 and had spent much of the war serving abroad. He had taken over the command of the Squadron in the previous December.

Quite tragically his replacement as Squadron Commander, Wing Commander P.F. Dunham, D.F.C., was killed on 19th February whilst engaged over Wesel. By a cruel twist of fate he was flying the Lancaster, PD338 'WP-P', which had been the other Lancaster involved in the collision earlier in the month. Furthermore this was the only aircraft lost on three raids to Wesel on 16th, 17th and 19th. It was a town on the east bank of the Rhine and was then close to the battlefront and a centre of German troop reinforcements. The Group's crews would return to Wesel in about a month's time with quite dramatic results.

The month of February was, of course, memorable for Operation *Thunderclap*, which was a combined Allied air offensive when Berlin, Chemnitz, Dresden and Leipzig were listed as possible targets as well as 'associated cities where heavy attacks will cause great confusion in civilian evacuation from the Eastern Front and hamper movements of troop reinforcements from other fronts'. So it was that the now 'infamous' Dresden operation was approved and authorised at the highest political level; in fact, there had been a meeting of Churchill, Roosevelt and Stalin at Yalta from 4th to 14th February where no doubt the impending air offensive was discussed.

Modern historians have since used the Dresden operation particularly to castigate Air Chief Marshal Harris and by inference his faithful crews. This is not the place to debate the moralities of 'area bombing'; the facts are that Dresden was a major rail and road centre used for troop reinforcements and supplies to the Eastern Front and therefore at this stage of the war it could be considered a legitimate strategic target. The U.S.A.A.F. had planned a daylight operation on 13th February, which was cancelled because of 'inferior weather'. Thus on the night of 13/14th eight hundred and four Lancasters and Mosquitos attacked Dresden in two waves, three hours apart, with No 3 Group's Lancasters in the second wave. Over two thousand, six hundred tons of bombs were dropped, which created a firestorm similar to that at Hamburg in late July 1943. Of the seven Lancasters lost on the night, one came from No 186 Squadron at Stradishall and all the crew were killed. It should be noted that the U.S.A.A.F. bombed Dresden the next day and again on the 15th and 2nd March, but it is now accepted that most of the damage and the large loss of civilian lives were due to the R.A.F.'s night raid. On 14/15th the Command's crews attacked Chemnitz in continuation of Operation *Thunderclap* and although No 3 Group lost two Lancasters on this raid, neither was from the Suffolk squadrons.

It could well be argued that in March Bomber Command had finally attained its pinnacle of performance in its long war – 3rd/4th was the two thousandth night of the war and for over 70% of those nights the Command's crews had been in action. During March No 3 Group alone mounted sixteen daylight *G-H* operations and also its crews were in action with the Main Force on four occasions when Cologne, Dessau, Dortmund and Essen were the targets. On the 2nd Cologne received its final raid of the war from over eight hundred and fifty aircraft attacking the city in two waves. It was a hugely destructive operation, when according to an eyewitness '... great carpets of bombs fell on the city ...*Das war das Ende von Koln ...*'. That was certainly true because four days later Cologne was captured by American forces. In this raid one of No 622 Squadron's Lancasters was shot down; out of the eight airmen killed two were Canadians and one an Australian.

There then followed three heavy raids in a matter of three days – 11th to 13th – directed on Dortmund, Essen and Wuppertal by over two thousand, five hundred and forty crews, who dropped some ten thousand, six hundred and fifty tons of bombs for the loss of only five Lancasters (0.2%). It was a massive and staggering demonstration of the destructive power of Bomber Command, moreover it was proof of the complete air superiority it had finally achieved over the German air defences. Essen became the most bombed city in Germany; it now lay in utter ruins.

Earlier in March (9th), No 138 (Special Duties) Squadron arrived at Tuddenham from Tempsford; since its formation at Newmarket Heath in August 1941 it had been solely engaged on Resistance operations but from now on it would become a heavy bomber unit equipped with Lancasters. No 138 was the last squadron to join the Group's *G-H* Force which now totalled eleven squadrons. It was not until 29th March that the Squadron became operational when three crews bombed the Hermann Goering Benzol plant at Salzgitter to the north-east of Hannover. They all returned safely, actually, none of the one hundred and thirty Lancasters involved in the raid were lost.

On 19th March No 90 Squadron lost its last aircraft in action when its crews were engaged in a *G-H* operation to Gelsenkirchen, which was the seventh time it had been bombed in 1945. The town was a prime target with its several synthetic oil and Benzol plants; on this occasion the Consolidation Benzol works was the objective, as it had been on a number of previous occasions. The Squadron's Lancaster was hit by flak whilst approaching the aiming point and again shortly after completing its bombing run, but it was the flak damage sustained on its return flight that gave Pilot Officer J.W. Price no alternative but to attempt a forced-landing in Allied-occupied Germany; it was successful and all the crew escaped without a single injury. A Lancaster of No 218 Squadron engaged in the same operation was also damaged by flak, but it made a successful emergency landing at Evere airfield in Brussels.

Three days later (22nd) No XV Squadron lost its last aircraft in action, bringing the total to one hundred and sixty-six whilst operating in Bomber Command. In the Squadron's long war (it had first served with the Advanced Air Striking Force in 1939) it had carried out six hundred and six bombing operations, one of the highest totals in the whole of the Command. This final Lancaster was lost in a most unfortunate manner. It took off from Mildenhall bound for the rail and road communications at Bocholt, about thirty miles north of the Ruhr Valley. Within minutes of leaving the airfield it crashed in flames near Mudford, Norfolk due to an engine fire and all seven airmen were killed.

One of the *G-H* Force's most successful operations came on 23rd March when eighty Lancasters attacked Wesel, an area soon to be attacked by the British land forces. The crews' bombing had to be accurate because the British troops were less than a mile away from the target area. The town was bombed again on the same night and after the two operations it was estimated that 97% of the buildings had been destroyed. On the morning of the 24th the Rhine was crossed and what was left of Wesel was captured by British troops a few hours later. Field Marshal Montgomery sent a message of thanks to Air Chief Marshal Harris on the excellence of the Command's precise bombing.

After the previous comments about mid-air collisions of 'friendly' aircraft, it has been reckoned that no less than forty-five aircraft were lost in this manner in 1945, which caused the deaths of over two hundred and fifty airmen. Included in this total was a Lancaster of No 186 Squadron which collided with a Lancaster of No 115 Squadron whilst outward bound to the oil installations at Leuna on 4/5th April, when only one of the sixteen airmen escaped. On the same operation another of the Squadron's Lancasters lost one of its engines due to flak, a second engine cut out and the aircraft crash-landed in a field adjacent to the airfield; quite miraculously all the crew survived the crash. For his flying skill and expertise the pilot, Flight Lieutenant Field, D.F.C., was awarded an 'immediate' Bar to his D.F.C.

Nine nights later (13/14th) Stradishall was the scene of another tragic incident when two of No 186 Squadron's aircraft, having safely returned from bombing U-boat pens at Kiel, collided whilst circling the airfield prior to landing; only three of the fourteen airmen survived. These were the last aircraft lost by the Squadron; in the rather brief time that it had been operational over one thousand and fifty sorties had been flown, but in the process twelve Lancasters had been lost, a relatively high loss at this stage of the war.

The following night, Bomber Command mounted its last major raid against a German city when Potsdam on the outskirts of Berlin was the target for five hundred Lancasters and twelve Mosquitos. It was the first time since March 1944 that heavy bombers had entered the Berlin defence zone, although of course Mosquitos of the Command's Light Night Striking Force had been bombing Berlin almost nightly. The precise targets this night were the centre of Potsdam, the large Army barracks and the railway centre. It was a successful operation with only two Lancasters lost but one of these belonged to No 138 Squadron, shot down by a night fighter; one of the last Lancasters to fall to the *Luftwaffe*. This was the only Lancaster the Squadron lost in eight bombing raids.

It was now clear that the end of the war was close at hand and on 16th April, Group Captain Ken S. Batchelor, D.F.C., MiD, who was the 'Station Master' at Mildenhall, felt he could spare the time to fly to Juvincourt in France to be formally presented with the *Croix de Guerre*. Batchelor had joined the R.A.F. in 1934 and was posted to No 9 Squadron before the outbreak of war. He had taken part in the first bombing raid on 4th September 1939 whilst with the Squadron at Honington. He later commanded No 311 (Czechoslovak) Squadron and in February 1943 he took over No 138 (Special Duties) Squadron and made many flights supplying arms and ammunition to the Resistance in enemy-occupied countries, hence the award of the *Croix de Guerre*. Batchelor had been appointed Station Commander at Mildenhall in December 1944. At that stage of the war he was just one of the many very experienced airmen who had flown countless operations and survived and completed their war as Station Commanders. He left Mildenhall in September 1945 and finally retired from the R.A.F. in 1964. He died in February 1994 aged eighty-seven years.

The last time Bomber Command was called upon to provide air support for the British land forces was on 22nd April when over seven hundred and sixty crews from four Bomber Groups attacked the south-eastern suburbs of Bremen, which was to be attacked by British troops two days later. Two Lancasters were lost and both came from Suffolk squadrons – Nos 622 and 218; this was the fifty-first and last aircraft lost by No 622 Squadron during the war.

Quite remarkably there were two Lancasters flying from Mildenhall on this Bremen raid that had completed over one hundred operations. It was rather extraordinary because only thirty-five individual Lancasters managed to achieve the 'magical century'. One of the Lancasters was LL885 'GI-J *Jig*' of No 622 Squadron, which was on its one hundred and fourteenth operation, but that figure was comfortably exceeded by LL806 'LS-J *Jig*' of No XV Squadron by twenty more operations. This Bremen raid was the last bombing operation of the war for Mildenhall. Perhaps more than any other bomber the Lancaster epitomised Bomber Command during the last three years of the war, and many veteran pilots still maintain that 'it was the best plane I ever flew'. Out of the five thousand, nine hundred and forty four-engine bombers the Command lost in action, 58% (3,431) were Lancasters and the loss rate of 2.2% was lower than either the Stirling or Halifax.

Two days later (24th) Chedburgh mounted its last bombing operation

Lancaster – LL806 'LS-J Jig' *– of No XV Squadron.* (via H.A. Butler)

'Jig's' *134 bombing operations are displayed along with three* Manna *and three* Exodus *operations.* (via H.A. Butler)

when eighteen Lancasters of No 218 Squadron left to bomb the railway yards at Bad Oldesloe and sadly there was a tragic accident. One of the Lancasters suffered engine failure whilst taking off, crashed on the edge of the airfield and exploded with a total loss of life. It proved to be a rather sad end for this wartime airfield.

Although the bombing war was over for No 3 Group and its squadrons, over the next week or so the crews were engaged on some pleasurable and satisfying operations codenamed *Manna*. This was the supply of food to the starving people of western Holland, which was still in enemy hands. The local German Commander had agreed a truce to allow food supplies to be dropped at several designated airfields and the racecourse at The Hague. In total, over two thousand, eight hundred Lancasters were engaged in these *Manna* drops delivering some six thousand, six hundred tons of food.

Also during this period (and beyond) the Lancaster crews were engaged in Operation *Exodus*, the early evacuation of freed prisoners of war from airfields in Belgium and France. Each Lancaster was able to carry twenty-four passengers and by 7th May a total of seventy-two thousand POWs had been brought home safely, a remarkable total in such a short period of time. Well after VE Day (8th May) the Lancaster squadrons were still ferrying POWs back home.

The last heavy bomber operation was mounted by the Command on 25/26th April but its final bombing operation took place on 2nd/3rd May when Mosquitos attacked the port of Kiel. This brought Bomber Command's long and harsh war to an end. No other Allied force had operated for such a prolonged length of time; its crews had been in action for 71% of the total nights and slightly over 50% of the days. During this time Bomber Command's aircrew casualties totalled seventy-three thousand, seven hundred and forty-one, which was nearly 60% of the airmen that served in the Command. It had been a monumental effort by the Command's aircrew and they all truly deserve the country's highest praise and honour.

Very appropriately this photograph of a Lancaster of No 149 Squadron brings Suffolk's wartime bomber story to a conclusion. Like so many other Lancasters, it was engaged on Operation Exodus. *(via J. Adams)*

Chapter 12

Remembering
'A Duty Nobly Done'

Sixty-three years have elapsed since Bomber Command's interminable and costly air offensive came to a merciful end and those survivors of what has been called 'an extraordinary and controversial story' are now a rapidly dwindling band of 'heroes', although none that I have been fortunate to meet would describe themselves as such. They felt that they were merely 'doing their duty' – nothing more and nothing less.

On 10th May 1945 Air Chief Marshal Sir Arthur Harris issued a Special Order of the Day, wherein he conveyed his appreciation to all those who had served under his command:

> To you who survived, I would say this. Content yourself, and take credit with those that perished and now that the 'Cease Fire' has sounded countless homes within our Empire will welcome back a father, husband or son whose life, but for your endeavours and your sacrifices, would assuredly have been expended during long further years of agony to achieve a victory already ours. No Allied Nation is clear of this debt to you.

Although Winston Churchill's VE Address to the Nation three days later did not contain any reference to the six-year bombing campaign, he did later famously acknowledge that 'the massive achievements by Bomber Command will long be remembered as an example of a duty nobly done'.

It is perhaps only in the last ten to fifteen years that there have been a number of published works that have finally recognised the immense contribution made by the 'Bomber Men' to the ultimate victory in Europe, sadly too late for many of the survivors.

Over the last sixty or so years these Bomber Command veterans have seen the demise of so many of their squadrons in which they served with distinction and pride. Of those bomber squadrons that flew from the Suffolk airfields only Nos 9 and 15 (Reserve) remain in the modern R.A.F. They have also witnessed the criticism and condemnation of the Chief, Sir Arthur Harris and his prosecution of the bombing offensive, but even today all are staunchly loyal to him and his memory. However, they did gain some satisfaction when a statue of him was erected in the precinct of the R.A.F.'s church, St Clement Dane in London; it was unveiled on 31st May 1992, eight years after his death in April 1984 aged eighty-one years. The statue is dedicated to all the men of Bomber Command as well as Air Chief Marshal Sir Arthur Harris.

These 'Bomber Men' have found comfort and solace in the numerous Squadron Associations, where at least once a year they could renew old friendships with fellow crew members and squadron colleagues, many of whom had travelled from distant Commonwealth countries to attend these emotional reunions. In 1985 the Bomber Command Association was formed and one of its aims is 'a means of continuing the comradeship that had been forged in the heat of battle and perpetuating the Command's history with truth, dignity and pride'. It is still a flourishing Association twenty-three years later.

Unlike those fighter pilots who flew in the Battle of Britain, there is no National Memorial dedicated to the airmen of Bomber Command, a rather sad and sorry omission, especially when compared to the fine memorial at Nanton Lancaster Air Museum in Canada for those Canadian airmen that lost their lives in Bomber Command. However, on 27th August 2006, a ledgerstone was unveiled at Lincoln Cathedral dedicated 'to the men of Bomber Command 1939-45 over 55,000 of whom gave their lives in defence of our liberty'.

How are all those 'Bomber Men' that flew from the Suffolk airfields remembered locally? Perhaps more than any other 'bomber county', Suffolk has a number of operational airfields that recall those dark days of the Second World War. The most famous one, of course, is Mildenhall, which is still very active seventy-four years since its opening. Lakenheath and Wattisham are still open for flying and Honington is the R.A.F.'s main centre for Force Protection, the home of the R.A.F. Regiment. Chedburgh was the first wartime airfield to close – in December 1946 – and very little of it remains today. Newmarket Heath was returned to its former owners, the Stewards of the Jockey Club, at the end of 1947. Tuddenham and Stradishall managed to survive rather longer; Tuddenham closed in July 1963 but Stradishall remained as a flying training station until the mid-1970s and the airfield site is now H.M. Highpoint Prison.

There are memorial stained-glass windows in the Base Chapel at Mildenhall and one below the bell tower in St Margaret's church, Stradishall. Besides the two memorials in St John's church, Beck Row and St Mary's church, Tuddenham previously noted, there are several memorials dotted around the county. At Newmarket Heath there is a fine propeller memorial to No 99 Squadron. The propeller belonged to a Wellington of the Squadron – T2886 – which crashed near Wisbech in February 1941; it was uncovered in 1982 and mounted on a concrete block and the memorial was dedicated in September 1985. There is also a memorial to the members of No 90 Squadron on the village green at Tuddenham and another on the perimeter of the old airfield which was unveiled in 1992. Two years later a fine memorial stone was unveiled at Stradishall. Chedburgh also has a plain and simple memorial dedicated to all those who served at this bomber station. Two village signs at Chedburgh and Stradishall proudly proclaim their historic links with the R.A.F. and Bomber Command.

Although the majority of airmen that lost their lives whilst serving in Bomber Command are buried in the various war cemeteries in Germany, there are seventy-six airmen buried in the military cemetery at the rear of St John's church, Beck Row. But those airmen that have no known graves are commemorated at the splendid Commonwealth Air Forces' Runnymede Memorial at Cooper's Hill, Surrey; over twenty thousand, four hundred and fifty names are listed and the majority are Bomber Command airmen.

But perhaps the most appropriate and 'living' memorial to all those 'Bomber Men' is the Lancaster – PA474 *The Phantom of the Ruhr* – of the Battle of Britain Memorial Flight. Just to see it and to hear the unmistakable sound of its Merlin engines brings memories flooding back of those long-lost days and nights of Bomber Command. This aircraft is a poignant reminder of the sacrifice, courage and utter determination of the 'Bomber Men', who should never be forgotten.

A montage of Suffolk memorials: 1. Newmarket Heath; 2. Chedburgh; 3. Stradishall; 4. Tuddenham St Mary.

The memorial cemetery in St John's churchyard, Beck Row.

*The 'Bomber Men's'
most appropriate and
tangible memorial
– Lancaster PA474 The
Phantom of the Ruhr
of the Battle of Britain
Memorial Flight.*

Bibliography

The undermentioned books relate to Bomber Command and some of the squadrons that served at Suffolk airfields.

Air Ministry, *Bomber Command*, H.M.S.O., 1941

Air Ministry, *Bomber Command Continues*, H.M.S.O., 1942

Ashworth, Chris, *R.A.F. Bomber Command, 1936-1968*, Patrick Stephens, 1993

Barker, Ralph, *The Thousand Plan: The Story of the First Thousand Bomber Raid on Cologne*, Chatto and Windus, 1965

Bowman, Martin W., *Mildenhall: Bombers, Blackbirds and the Boom Years*, Tempus Pub., 2007

Bowyer, Chaz, *Bomber Barons*, William Kimber, 1983

Bowyer, Michael, *2 Group: A Complete History, 1936-1945*, Faber & Faber, 1974

Bowyer, Michael, *The Stirling Story*, Crecy Pub., 2001

Chorley, W.R., *R.A.F. Bomber Command Losses in the Second World War*, Vols 1-5, Midland Publications, 1992-1998

Cooper, Alan W., *Air Battle of the Ruhr*, Airlife, 1992

Cooper, Alan W., *Bombers Over Berlin: The R.A.F. Offensive November 1943-March 1944*, William Kimber, 1985

Delve, Ken, *Bomber Command 1936-1968: An Operational and Historical Record*, Pen and Sword, 2005

Delve, Ken & Jacobs, P., *The Six Year Offensive*, Arms and Armour, 1992

Edgerley, Squadron Leader A.G. (compiler), *Each Tenacious: A History of No 99 Squadron (1917-1976)*, Square One, 1993

Embry, Sir Basil, *Mission Completed*, Methuen, 1957

Falconer, Jonathan, *Bomber Command Handbook*, Sutton Publishing, 1998

Falconer, Jonathan, *Bomber Command: In Fact, Film and Fiction*, Sutton Publishing, 1996

Ford-Jones, M., *Bomber Squadron: The Men Who Flew With XV*, William Kimber, 1987

Franks, Norman, *Forever Strong: The Story of No 75 R.N.Z.A.F.*, Random House, 1991

Harris, Sir Arthur, *Bomber Offensive*, Collins, 1947

Jackson, R., *Before the Storm: The Story of Bomber Command, 1939-1942*, Arthur Barker, 1972

Longmate, Norman, *The Bombers: The R.A.F. Offensive Against Germany, 1939-1945*, Hutchinson, 1983

Middlebrook, Martin, *The Battle of Hamburg*, Allen Lane, 1980

Middlebrook, Martin, *The Berlin Raids*, Viking, 1988

Middlebrook, Martin, *The Bomber Command Diaries*, Viking, 1985

Middlebrook, Martin, *The Nuremberg Raid, 30-31 March 1944*, Penguin, 1973

Middlebrook, Martin & Everitt, Charles, *An Operational Reference Book, 1939-45*,

Neillands, Robin, The *Bomber War: Arthur Harris and the Allied Strategic Bombing Offensive, 1939-1945*, John Murray, 2001

Overy, Richard, *Bomber Command, 1939-45: Reaping the Whirlwind*, Harper Collins, 1996

Revie, Alastair, *The Lost Command*, David Bruce and Watson, 1971

Richards, Denis, *The Hardest Victory: R.A.F. Bomber Command in the Second World War*, Hodder and Stoughton, 1994

Searby, John H., *The Great Raid: Peenemünde – 17th August 1943*, Nutshell Press, 1978

Smith, Graham, *Suffolk Airfields in the Second World War*, Countryside Books, 1995

Taylor, G., *Operation Millennium: Bomber Harris's Raid on Cologne, May 1942*, Robert Hale, 1987

Warner, Graham, *The Bristol Blenheim: A Complete History*, Crecy Pub., 2002

Webster, Sir Charles & Frankland, Noble, *The Strategic Air Offensive against Germany, 1939-45*, 4 Volumes, H.M.S.O., 1961

Index